GOD AT WORK
IN ISRAEL

GOD at Work in ISRAEL

GERHARD VON RAD

TRANSLATED BY
JOHN H. MARKS

ABINGDON
Nashville

Library of Congress Cataloging in Publication Data

RAD, GERHARD VON. 1901-1971.
      God at work in Israel.
      Translation of Gottes Wirken in Israel.
      Includes bibliographical references.
      1. Bible. O.T.—Criticism, interpretation, etc.—
      Addresses, essays, lectures. I. Title.
      BS1192.R3213   221.6   79-26281

ISBN 0-687-14960-6

MANUFACTURED BY THE PARTHENON PRESS AT
NASHVILLE, TENNESSEE, UNITED STATES OF AMERICA

CONTENTS

TRANSLATOR'S PREFACE

Translated in this volume are nineteen lectures of Gerhard von Rad, who lived from 1901 to 1971, on the Old Testament. He delivered them in an effort to make the Old Testament more widely known to an interested but ill-informed public. The lectures are therefore neither technical nor abstruse, but are what he called "critical paraphrases."

The lectures are presented here in two groups. The first contains critical paraphrases of biblical passages; the second comprises lectures in which the biblical texts are considered thematically. An effort has been made to retain the original, oral style in the translation. The title for the collection was given by the German publisher. Notes to each lecture give the date of composition, the place of first delivery, and, if it was published, the place of publication.

1

HOW TO READ
THE OLD TESTAMENT

The Bible remains a bestseller, but in our western civilization there are probably few who read the Bible with passion. Many are fascinated with this book, in one way or another—there are so many ways!—yet they are not very disturbed when they do not quite comprehend what they are reading. Among such readers we may find not a few poets and literary epicures.

What the Bible means to people has varied markedly. In the world of the early medieval monasteries, men took up the Bible fully prepared to concentrate on it and stay with it completely, to apply every conceivable effort to it. Those who copied it in the quiet of their cells celebrated this book with unprecedented beauty of calligraphy and pictorial illumination. Today, in general, one takes up the Bible with more restraint and reservation, perhaps with a remarkable combination of respect and helplessness. For those who like to read, it is a marginal book. The truth is that the best read and most cultivated among us are scarcely familiar with it any more. H. V. Hofmannsthal once heard a passage from second Isaiah read at a party. Impressed with what he had heard, he went home, looked in vain through his Bible for the book, and then wrote a friend that he could not find "second Isaiah" in his Bible.

In the centuries after the Reformation, the Bible became for the first time a household book, an individual and family possession of culture and refinement. Before that, of course, the entire western world had used the Bible in every area of its life. Century after century it took from the

Bible what it needed not only for its religious life, but also for its law, science, and art, without exhausting the biblical resource. But in the post-Reformation period Bible stories were read aloud at home and became the cultural possession of the masses. Even today, the simplest man who knows his Bible may be considered educated in the best sense of the word. There are, after all, six world empires with which the Bible is concerned over a period of more than fourteen centuries. It mentions the most ancient empires of the Egyptians and Babylonians. The Assyrians almost destroyed Israel on her own turf, but the Bible follows with keen interest the break-up of Semitic world rule and the transfer of "empire" to the Indo-Europeans. It observes the fall of the Persian empire and, with the coming of the Greeks, the spread of Hellenism. The New Testament, finally, stands against the historical horizon of a world at peace because of Roman rule. But the Bible contains not only history, but legal material, varieties of prayer, and even love poetry. Now, the Bible has long since lost this position as fount of comfort and instruction, as foundation of all culture and education. The interesting conclusion of linguists is that the disappearance of biblical material has noticeably narrowed the range of our daily speech, which in turn has made Bible-reading more difficult.

On the other hand, modern biblical science has revealed so much material that is new, exciting, and of immediate interest, that we have no grounds for gloom. This book owes its existence to the desire to present the Bible in this relatively new light. To be sure, the Bible never was easy reading; and the finest interpretation cannot and should not make it so. Whatever one wrote in ancient Israel, it was not for speed-reading. But much can be done, nevertheless, to remove difficulties from the way of the modern reader for whom the Bible is strange so that its passages again become as direct and engaging as they in fact are and as they have been understood again and again at great hours in the history of Christianity. Part of that effort to remove difficulties is to make the reader aware of important matters that he must at first simply accept, if he is to read with understanding. Because today so many are baffled by those matters, we will discuss them at once.

Above all else, whoever studies the Old Testament must read with firm intent and not be satisfied with general feelings or impressions. Those who are hard to satisfy, who want to know precisely, who want to understand in detail what is being said, will read with more comprehension. The passages in the Old Testament are usually so striking in their diction that they wait for just such readers. Place names too may not be passed over. Hölderlin in his poems moves familiarly through the landscapes of Greece, without having been there. How much more must the Bible reader do likewise! Often proper understanding of a story depends on knowing where the place is and what peculiarities are connected with it. Only a patient effort at familiarizing oneself with these facts will clarify the narratives or Psalms or prophetic sermons, as the case may be. The profile of the passages will become sharper, and the reader will be more and more able to distinguish the enormous differences in the literary types which he meets as he reads.

One will easily distinguish a genealogy from a collection of legal axioms, but one must also distinguish carefully between narratives. One story will follow the course of events as objectively and compactly as a newsreel; another, likewise devoted compactly to an event, seeks to encounter the reader. It does not want to inform him, but rather to encounter him in the depths of his own relationship to God and cause him to ponder. A third is unmistakably didactic; it suggests norms for behavior, summons a reader to action, and wants to drive him to a kind of imitation. All such teaching narratives, however, which address the reader above and beyond their material, belong to later times. Much more characteristic in the writing of early Israel is the opposite, namely, the narrator's complete withdrawal from those events with which every Bible reader must come to grips. In most of the patriarchal narratives, already with Abraham and altogether with Jacob, the reader feels himself left completely in the lurch by the narrator. He wants earnestly to learn from him what was good and true in the acts and non-acts of the characters and what was bad and false. But the narrator tells him nothing. That is intended to show him not to be so hasty in judging the characters in these stories. Rather, he is to pay attention to what God has let happen to them. To be sure, one whose perception is finely tuned will recognize the light and shaded sides in the actions of those men whom God had encountered. This often puzzling imperturbability in the narrator, which is anything but unconcern, must be understood first. Many of these narratives are, in addition, products of a determined intent at art and were in those days certainly evaluated as works of art. Here, indeed, we have a remarkably paradoxical fact whose joy every reader of the Bible knows. The more we return the material first to its ancient milieu, which is far removed from us, the clearer and more interesting it becomes.

But the narrative literature, which occupies so much space in the Old Testament, demands even more of the modern reader. Israel worked more intensively than any other ancient people with her own history. The various documents from which the Pentateuch is put together and the whole story of David's accession to the throne as well as the deuteronomistic and finally the late historical work of the Chronicler, demonstrate how Israel from time to time went back afresh to write her history. These great literary works often took a century to mature to their final form or to be framed ingeniously with others by editors, so that in the end they became mighty, misshapen collections that were scarcely still considered literature for reading. To help the modern reader unravel such material is one of the primary tasks of this book.

The Old Testament unfolds a panorama of history with such detailed description that a reader educated in the western world feels at first engaged. Intensive study of history and the analysis of great historical works are indeed not new to him. He can participate in that. In fact, no other people of the ancient Near East has provided the modern historian with such an abundance of excellent source material. Israel's history, with all its effective political, social, and religious forces, can be reconstructed with more precision than that of any other ancient people. But having said that, we must also say that modern interest in history is completely different from that which bound Israel to her history. For Israel that interest was not a thirst for knowledge that happened to be concentrated on history; for in history, as nearly every page of the Old Testament affirms, Israel encountered her God. Let it be understood: this encounter was not accessible to Israel in a one-time historical document as though chiseled in stone, but rather in the leadings, callings, promises, and judgments that each generation had to ponder afresh. Israel had to let herself be addressed directly by the events of her history, in their constantly changing shape. That was the reason for her alternating efforts to represent anew great stretches of her history. The Old Testament is to a great extent nothing but the literary record of a people's passionate millennium-long conversation about the meaning of its history. In Israel too, the spirit of the times changes with time. The perceptions of earlier generations ceased to satisfy. History had to be understood and appropriated against a horizon of perception that was in a state of constant change. If, for example, one age perceived God's activity primarily in outside interferences in history, in miracles, or in the precipitate call of men to be God's instruments, another age saw God's activity bordering on the invisible, worked effectually into the chain of men's actions. Although Israel, in her great and long-time struggle over the meaning of her history, was not granted an unambiguous answer and a conclusive perception, she did speak in incomparable depth and breadth about God in her historical representations.

The man of today is able to deal with history in a masterly way and to interpret it, be it for winning insights or for conversation. This maneuverability in dealing with history provides no advantage for understanding the Old Testament. In fact it is likely to be a serious hindrance. One current view of history is prejudicially stamped by knowledge about the distance of the past from the present. It consciously thinks of history in terms of distance. It examines its transmitted witnesses, but it reserves its own judgment about the period. Thereby it expresses a feeling of superiority that, in the final analysis, is a feeling of superiority the living have over the dead. Today one can do everything with the historical. One can lift something from this world of the dead into the light of the living, to be amused by it; one can change it or one can also forget it. It is all at one's pleasure.

Israel's relationship to her history was diametrically opposed to that. She was remarkably unable to forget the events of her history and to take leave of the past. We can be certain that she herself would gladly have forgotten not a little. We have already referred to the way she again and again introduced her past into her present. The book of Deuteronomy is unanimously considered to be a relatively recent work. It is a long valedictory of Moses before his people. Those who composed it in this form did not consider themselves to be guilty of some pious fraud and were not using a literary artifice either. Moses' voice, as it was heard in their imaginations in the late royal era, went forth to this declining period, taking account of its specific troubles and grappling with the disorder of its religious and social life. Over a distance of many centuries past it was possible once again to stand at the foot of Mt. Sinai and hear God's will. Thus Israel introduced her divine history into the present! Perhaps we may express it better by saying that history itself intruded again and again into Israel. It was not Israel's free will at all to identify herself in this way with her history. History arose and addressed her. When a generation in Israel occupied itself with its history, it occupied itself with its own relationship to God.

One must learn as a reader to accompany ancient Israel in this most important matter, to accept this as the primary concern of the Old Testament writings. Often enough that will mean seeing the finger of history pointing to God for the first time. Not everywhere will the reader have such an easy time as he does in the Joseph story, where the narrator at the climax of the events lets Joseph speak the explanatory words (Gen. 50:20). Other patriarchal stories seem at first glance to be very reserved, and yet how silhouetted and compactly they make the "proclamation"! In that word the reader cannot escape God. And if he does manage to slip over it, if in this matter he succeeds cleverly in evading the encounter, then he has missed everything else as well.

The Old Testament is committed to speak about God in no particular method or manner. On the contrary, its possibilities of expression extend from most devout submission all the way to an almost blasphemous parody of everything that is considered holy (in Job and some of the prophets). One will with difficulty find words that surpass in fervor and strength those that are used in many psalms to address or speak about God. But in contrast to this language of prayer, that developed its concentrated form over many centuries, are other words about God which anticipate in sovereign fashion almost everything that would later be said by deniers and enemies of God. For the normal, devout Israelite too, there existed a kind of divine code of honor, i.e., definite conceptions about what one could entrust and not entrust to God, how one should and should not speak of him. But the prophets did not adhere to that code at all. They often spoke in downright scandalous language about God, and it is quite clear that they wanted thereby as iconoclasts to destroy conventional ideas about God. Why did they do that? They did not do it in strong reforming zeal, i.e., with the intention of putting talk about God upon more realistic ground. They were not reformers and did not think that their language about God would become the general style of speaking about him. Their reasons were different, and here we touch upon some of the hardest burdens Israel had to bear. Abraham, Moses, and the prophets had to drive home with force what was always the same and always new: Precisely when God revealed

15

himself to them, he at the same time concealed himself in incomprehensibility more profoundly than before. Is it not essentially everywhere the same? When one thinks and awaits God, light must dawn and the holy occur; and earthly confusion must be overcome in the marvel of deity. When God drew near to Israel, however, he destroyed all human ideas and images and often enough thrust Israel out into new temptations. The sacrifice of Isaac, "I am who I am" (Exod. 3:14), the command to Isaiah that he make his people obdurate (6:10)—is there not in the delineation of all these great, revelatory experiences at first more darkness than light? And are they all not simply steps toward the extraordinary suggestion of the New Testament that God in the cross of Christ drew very near to man and therein concealed himself more profoundly than men have ever thought bearable?

That was the way of the God with whom Israel had conversation, yielding herself to him, rising up against him, and again returning to him; always, however, in conversation with him and not released from that even in the darkest hours.

Let us finally look briefly at the human partners. What does the one who stands opposite God look like? He would be a poor Bible reader indeed, who would not be fascinated by this incomparable picture book of undisguised humanity. Everything is represented there, the lofty and the low, the terrible and the pure. These kings and soldiers, princes and bankrupts, men of God and unforgettable women—they all bustle about on the most human of all stages. What composure in describing even the darkest matters! To see man in this way means, you must know, that God has seen him beforehand. In this long coversation of a people with God—think of the Psalter!—not only is God revealed, man too is revealed to himself, more clearly than he could have seen himself by himself. Only in God's light does man come into his true size; here alone does he become great and inscrutable; here only does he release all the possibilities of his own self-understanding. In the Old Testament he becomes known to himself as a creature, who, whether he knows it or not, is in partnership with God; a creature who is drawn into a vast divine story and who, designed as he is from the beginning for conversation with God, needs to be addressed by God in the events of his life under all circumstances. By that word he lives, with it he stands, and without it he falls.

Here too there is much obscure along with what is clear. The riddles of suffering, indeed the terrors of being forsaken by God, are seen in full awareness and honesty, even as their solutions are sought. The question indeed is raised whether the suffering of God's people may not be more than a just and passing punishment, may not be a vicarious service which this people alone must perform. This question too is not clearly answered in all of the Old Testament. The enigma of Israel's history retains its same urgency in New Testament thought. It stands over Jesus' conversation with his contemporaries, and is present more than ever in the fateful separation of the young Christian community from the Jewish synagogue after the Christians, in the confidence of being the true Israel, began to regard the life and death of Jesus of Nazareth as the final fulfillment of God's history with Israel and to interpret the entire Old Testament from the perspective of the Easter event. Finally, one cannot possibly understand the appearance of modern Israel without detailed knowledge of the questions and expectations of this book that is so many millennia old.

The purpose of these lines was to advise the reader of some things he must first accept as given before he determines to take it upon himself to read and hear the Old Testament. Of course he is not to be prevented from freely taking a stand on what he has read. Neither is he to think that he should at once appropriate what he has read and certainly not that he should repeat it as his own. He will, however, be well-advised to take time before he passes judgment on it, to learn to read with a deep breath as it were, and to discipline himself in reserving his doubts and objections, which he will certainly have, for a

17

later time. Reading the Bible has always demanded that one be prepared for contemplation.

A final word. This book, to the study of which the reader is now dismissed, is rather special in not being, like many others, a book "about" the Old Testament. It will not give information about what biblical scholars today think about this text or that sphere of ideas. This book will not inform at all. What it offers of science is meant to teach one to see more clearly the demand of truth in a biblical text or group of texts. It attempts to remove hindrances from the way of a true encounter with the message of a biblical passage. If the reader is successful in keeping himself prepared for such an encounter and free from the false notion that he already knows what he is going to read, he will perceive more and more clearly that the biblical text is itself concerned with him. Then his reading will be on the right track.

2

THE STORY OF JOSEPH

(First published as Heft 5 of Biblische Studien, *Neukirchener Verlag, Neukirchen-Vluyn, 1954 [4th ed. 1964].)*

Biblical science has long since determined that the Joseph story in the Old Testament has been very cleverly put together from two earlier versions. The fine seams that are everywhere apparent to the scholar scarcely come to the attention of the untutored reader, and so he reads with incomparably greater profit than annoyance. Indeed the narrative owes its charming inner spaciousness and its whole richness of scenes, motifs, and problems directly to its careful composition.

For us, however, who approach this story from a great distance, there is something else to consider. We know today all kinds of stories, so whoever writes today has a multitude of models which he can cultivate and by which he can be guided. In ancient Israel the situation was quite different. There, bookshops stacked to the roof with novels did not exist. The ancients, indeed, wrote far less than we do, and when they did write, it was at far greater intellectual and spiritual cost. Theirs was in fact a hazardous enterprise, an adventure of the mind. Problems of a story's form and the possibilities of presentation had to be resolved without the aids available to modern narrators. Certainly that was true of the Joseph story, for we can say with assurance that it arose in its present form without any models that could have been decisive for it.

That means, then, that we have to examine and interpret it differently from the way we would treat the latest work of Ernest Hemingway. The difference is that such stories originally appeared in a large, empty, intellectual room, and so we also have to put aside from the beginning every feeling of ostensible familiarity.

It may therefore be permissible to approach the matter from a completely external conclusion: Almost all the narratives in the book of Genesis are limited to a definite length of some twenty to thirty verses. The Joseph story vastly exceeds those limits. It contains 392 verses and is still *one* narrative and not a wreath of individual stories complete in themselves. None of its chapters can be understood apart from the whole. How different that is from the stories of Isaac's sacrifice, God's visit to Mamre, and others! The Joseph story, as a narrative, is a unity with a single suspense-curve and one climax, at most two. How much longer is its path from "the exciting moment," which occurs in every proper story, to the denouement! Every attentive reader knows the suspense with which he awaits the actual outcome, but it keeps being postponed. That itself shows that the story, both in its essence and its origin, is something different in the history of literature from the stories about Abraham and Jacob.

The Joseph story differs from the other patriarchal stories also in the fact that its central character is unambiguously clear. Abraham's character is ambiguous enough, to say nothing of Jacob's. The stories of Abraham or Jacob only seldom want to depict model characters, as has been sufficiently stated already. They depict, rather, men who have been seized by God's promise; they portray the most singular situations in which those men find themselves when the promise is in default, situations in which they go to pieces often enough. They also depict, however, the way in which God carries his promise over every human failure. I would even go so far as to say that one cannot speak at all, in the modern sense of the word, of a "character" Abraham in the stories about Abraham or Jacob. That is, the narrator is not really interested in the humanity of his "character" and does not want to sketch it. To be sure, Abraham's humanity comes into close contact with us in the story of his sacrifice of Isaac; but in the great number of these stories that is almost an exception, and it was not the narrator's primary purpose to occupy us with it. His primary purpose was to show how God's promise was obscured for Abraham, when God demanded the sacrifice of the son he had promised Abraham, and what the outcome of that terrible divine inconsistency could be. On the whole, Abraham and Jacob interest the narrator not as "characters," but as recipients of revelation and as men who were seized by God's plans. In the various situations and conflicts from story to story, the individual narratives show a different Abraham in each one.

All that is different in the Joseph story. Here we have a character, here the human is displayed from every angle, and not simply in one or more episodes. Rather, the narrator keeps this person in view throughout almost the entire span of his life. So mature is the interest of this story for the human as such that it compels one to say that the Joseph story must be emphatically and essentially distinguished from the patriarchal stories. It must, consequently, have its origin in a quite different intellectual and theological place.

We must now, therefore, define briefly the place and intellectual atmosphere in which this narrator lived. Every narrative is of course marked by the particular manner of thought of its narrator, and every narrator is in turn marked by the intellectual atmosphere in which he lives. Even if we consider him ever so "creative" from the standpoint of human productivity, he still lives and breathes as a religious narrator in the traditional or perhaps even revolutionary intellectual and theological perceptions of his time.

I

With the rise of her monarchy Israel found herself in profound crisis. The reign of Solomon was particularly drastic. Israel had now stepped out onto the political stage. She was drawn into international diplomacy; she maintained a standing army of mercenaries rather than drawing on a general levy of free peasants; she built garrisons for the corps of war chariots; the state undertook trade expeditions to distant lands; and a great bureaucratic apparatus began to take over the complex administration of this new government. All this was an upheaval that separated that era from the previous era of the Judges, and it brought about a profound internal and intellectual transformation. The ancient, sacred traditions of the distant past died out, and their literary heritage was carefully collected and edited. That itself is the sign of an end and of a relative conclusion to an era. Most important, however, the way in which faith had thought of God's effective action in history was replaced by quite new ideas. For example, in the past, the period of the Judges, Israel had seen God's activity as bound to the sacred institutions, to the cult and holy war, to the charisma of specially chosen men, and to miracles. How did the new age see God's rule in history? We will see. This Solomonic era was indeed an era of a risky rupture, but also of a brand new intellectual departure, a kind of enlightenment, i.e., a time when human self-consciousness and self-confidence were awakening. Men were conscious of their intellectual powers and their ability to marshall facts. New dimensions of their environment came into view, not least that of man himself, his psychological complexity and the enigmatic unfathomableness of his inner being. The appearance of these new dimensions made it possible to put on record in narrative form this whole world of the human. One can depict such a complicated affair as the beginning of the Joseph story—how the father, Jacob, receives news of the young Joseph's dreams, how he scolds the lad for his pride and still supports him and keeps the matter in mind. One can describe how Joseph comes in the morning to the chief officials of the prison and asks them, "Why are your faces downcast today?" This conversation's opener is itself a work of art. One should notice here the way in which the narrator leads from the external, the downcast faces, to the inner problem. One can picture the psychological effect of a surprising, stunning disclosure: the brothers, arriving home from Egypt, tell their father, "Joseph is still alive, and he is ruler over all the land of Egypt!" "And his heart fainted" (wayyafog libbo), "for he did not believe them." Above all, one should here read the description of the inner turmoil that broke out in Joseph when he saw Benjamin again after so many years.

And he inquired about their welfare, and said, "Is your father well, the old man of whom you spoke? Is he still alive?" They said, "Your servant our father is well, he is still alive." And they bowed their heads and made obeisance. And he lifted up his eyes, and saw his brother Benjamin, his mother's son, and said, "Is this your youngest brother, of whom you spoke to me? God be gracious to you, my son!" Then Joseph made haste, for his heart yearned for his brother, and he sought a place to weep. And he entered his chamber and wept there. Then he washed his face and came out; and controlling himself he said, . . ." (Gen. 43:27-31)

In this incomparable scene we feel in our bones the atmosphere of this audience. Joseph had just inquired again about his father, "Is your father well, the old man of whom you spoke?" The brothers answered stiffly with the very same words: "Your servant our father is well, he is still alive." With that the conversation again stops. The brothers bow their heads, and the room is again still. Everyone senses in the hesitating brothers the heaviness of heart in Joseph, for we read, when Joseph "lifted up his eyes, and saw his brother Benjamin" (he had, therefore, lowered his eyes), he asked, "Is this your youngest brother, of whom you spoke to me?" This is quite a different question from the first one which the brothers had answered respectfully. Joseph does not wait for their answer; he can evidently no longer keep his composure. He says quickly, "God be gracious to you, my son" and hastens from the room to weep.

The earlier narrators of the stories about Abraham did not know about such narrative possibilities. That was at that time new territory for a storyteller, and the freshness of this literary achievement still clings to the narrative. But what I just said about describing psychological matters is true in even a wider sense. One can detect in the Joseph story a secret joy in the coming into view of a broader horizon. Interpreters before us have already pointed to that enlightened interest in the customs and conditions of a foreign people, and we might say that the Joseph story exhibits a certain joy in the exotic: in the glittering Egyptian court, the installation of a vizier with whom strangers can do business only with the aid of an interpreter, the governmental storage of grain, the mumification of the dead, etc. What did the Israel of Gideon's day know of such things?

But we must return to the whole spirit of that enlightened epoch to which the narrator of our story belongs. That early, royal era had a definite ideal for education, and in that it was pioneering. It had in mind a definite, striking image of man, to which every young person should be educated to conform. That ideal of a young man, as it was understood in the narrator's time, is beautifully presented in the story where one of the court attendants of melancholy Saul recommends young David to him as a page: "Behold, I have seen a son of Jesse, the Bethlehemite, who is skillful in playing, a man of valor, a man of war, prudent in speech, and a man of good presence; and the Lord is with him" (I Sam. 16:18).

We have here a statement about the character and conduct of a young Israelite man in good favor. Presupposed is his membership in the class of free landowners; next to his skill in music is his military training; his good appearance recommends him; and he must above all command the art of speaking. The final and most important requirement cannot be learned; it is there, or it is not: namely, God's blessing. How close this is to the Joseph story, which tells of Joseph's beauty and skill in speaking and not least, though several times cryptically, that "the Lord was with Joseph." Our story, however, ranges much wider than does the short sketch about David.

But we have an even richer source for understanding this courtly ideal for education in the maxims of the older "wisdom" literature, for the education of eligible young men in the early, royal period was in the hands of the teachers of wisdom. The aphorisms of these wise men are frequently concerned with training boys when and when not to speak.

> The mind of the wise makes his speech judicious,
> and adds persuasiveness to his lips. (Prov. 16:23)
> Death and life are in the power of the tongue,
> and those who love it will eat its fruits. (Prov. 18:21)
> A soft tongue will break a bone. (Prov. 25:15)

They also teach emphatically the art of self-control:

> A tranquil mind gives life to the flesh,
> but passion makes the bones rot. (Prov. 14:30)
> He who is slow to anger has great understanding,
> but he who has a hasty temper exalts folly. (Prov. 14:29)

And they warn emphatically against "loose women":

> For a harlot is a deep pit; an adventuress in a narrow well.
> She lies in wait like a robber and increases the faithless
> among men. (Prov. 23:27-28)

For whom are these maxims intended, if they do not apply to Joseph? He is indeed the one "slow to anger" who "quiets contention" (Prov. 15:18). Of him it can also be said, "love covers all offenses" (Prov. 10:12). And the great temptation story, Joseph and Potiphar's wife, can be read as a direct illustration of the warning against loose women.

What is peculiar in this ideal of education is that it does not direct the young man toward religion, revelation, and faith, but rather addresses him from the fact of revelation. Fear of the Lord is the beginning of this education (Prov. 1:7; 15:33). Joseph too confesses this fear of God (Gen. 42:18). What is absent from this striving after education is the passion for redemption. Characteristic of it is its lack of rigidity and absence of the doctrinaire. Its deliberate consideration of the possible makes it distinctly realistic.

Special importance was attached to the art of well-constructed address. To make one able to speak well at critical moments was a major goal of this education. The concern was with political speaking, giving counsel in the affairs of the state; and the supreme goal was to receive a position near the king and serve him.

> Do you see a man skilful in his work?
> he will stand before kings. (Prov. 22:29)
> Do not neglect the studies of the learned . . . from these you will learn discipline, and how to be the servant of princes (Eccles. 8:8).

In matters of this worldly wisdom Israel had learned much from the ancient Egyptians, and it is fitting to quote at least one example of non-Israelite instruction:

> If thou art a man of standing, one sitting in the counsels of his lord, summon thy resources for good. If thou art silent, it is better than *teftef* plants. If thou speakest, thou shouldst know how thou canst explain (difficulties). It is a (real) craftsman who can speak in counsel, (for) speaking is more difficult than any labor. (*The Instruction of Ptah-hotep,* l. 365 c. 2350 B.C.)

The Old Testament has many fine examples of such speaking, which the modern reader usually passes over, but which the ancients knew how to treasure. There are none more eloquent than the two in Absalom's council of war, where Ahithophel and Hushai outline their plans for the war (II Sam. 17:1-23). But there is no need to seek examples elsewhere. The Joseph story itself has two. What Joseph does, when he has been brought from prison to the pharaoh, is exactly what the teachers of wisdom had trained him to do: he gives counsel in a well-constructed address (Gen. 41:25-36). Equally brilliant is Judah's speech, when the brothers' distress over Joseph's silver divining cup is most acute. It comes protractedly just before Joseph makes himself known to them. The narrator says, "Then Judah went up to him."

The moment is impressive. "O my lord, let your servant, I pray you, speak a word in my lord's ears, and let not your anger burn against your servant; for you are like Pharaoh himself" (Gen. 44:18-34). In this address the narrator has Judah put together all his skill that with noble words, understanding, and sensitivity he may master the terrible situation.

It is not only in the great speeches, however, but altogether in the fine art of delighting the reader here and there with a sparkling word that we recognize the influence of those teachers of wisdom. Think, for example, of that charming scene when in the morning the brothers, on their second visit to Egypt, are received by Joseph's kindly housekeeper and led into Joseph's private apartment. They find everything sinister, behave awkwardly, and act as men of low degree. Already at the door they begin to speak. Who knows all the whims of fortune that can befall one at a foreign court! The brothers imagine that a guard will leap out from somewhere and fall upon them. In their anxiety they speak far too much—an accurate psychological picture! And then, in answer to their worry about the money they had found in their sacks upon their last journey home, there comes that wonderfully ambiguous word of the housekeeper: "Rest assured, do not be afraid; God . . . must have put treasure in your sacks for you!" (Gen. 43:17-25). Can you not hear the teacher of wisdom saying: "A word fitly spoken is like apples of gold in a setting of silver" (Prov. 25:11). "He who gives a right answer kisses the lips" (Prov. 24:26).

II

We now turn first to the extraordinary manner of thinking that pervades the story of Joseph, which one must recognize in order to understand the story. What are its content and intent? What is the narrator's actual purpose? First, certainly, the intent is to present a young man who by discipline, modesty, knowledge, friendliness, self-control, and fear of God has given his whole being an excellent form, and who remains the same noble person in all situations, whether in misery or in splendor. But the intent is of course much more than that. As we now proceed to define its actual content, we must bear in mind that we will ruin the story if we characterize it ·merely as pious or edifying. It is not that at all, and in that respect it differs from the earlier patriarchal stories that spoke much more directly about God. Where in this story do we ever read a statement like "God appeared," "God spoke," "God again went up," "God gave heed," etc.? In comparison with all these older stories, the Joseph story is distinguished by a revolutionary worldliness, a worldliness that unfolds the entire realm of human life, with all its heights and depths, realistically and without miracle.

The arrangement of the massive material is quite evident. The first part, up to chapter 41, presents the drama of the external events: the sale of Joseph and his arrival in Egypt, Joseph in Potiphar's house, Joseph in prison, and finally his fabulous rise to power. The second part, from chapter 42 to the end, presents his meeting with his brothers, and with that the *inner* drama of the events becomes definitely prominent. God is mentioned in the first part too. As Joseph descends to his most abject humiliation, the reader learns more than once that "God was with Joseph" (Gen. 39:2, 21, 23). But in the pervading worldliness of the other events, these statements about God have an almost forlorn aspect. Of course, they are important enough. They do not mean that God preserved Joseph from suffering, but rather that he preserved him *in the midst* of suffering. Still, one must not perceive in them the real subject of the whole Joseph story. We come much closer to that in the interpretation of the dream, when Joseph is brought before the pharaoh. There the prisoner—quickly washed and dressed for the occasion— freely informs the pharaoh, who considers him to be a special diviner, that to reveal the mystery of the future can never be a matter of learning some art or technique. Indeed, Joseph tells him, he himself would have found the task impossible had not God granted illumination, for only the free God is lord of the future. Whoever talks about the future talks about God! This address, in which Joseph almost in terror rejects the pharaoh's demand and therewith most gravely endangers his own freedom, is a contribution to the discussion about the freedom of those who are bound.

The real subject of the Joseph story appears in full view only in the second part of the narrative. Here God is mentioned quite programmatically, but still only in two places, which shows a conspicuous economy, a theological reticence and modesty that characterize our story. As unquestionably decisive as may be what this narrator says of God and his part in the whole event, however, one must still remember that the human aspects of the moral conflicts interest him too. That is easy to show in the remarkably secular, apparently quite untheological way in which the problem of guilt pervades the whole story. The brothers commit the crime against Joseph, and the sanddrift of continuing events seems to rest on it for years. Then the brothers, who have come to Egypt, find themselves standing before a high official whom they do not know and who receives them harshly. In their story of their family conditions, the shadow of Joseph arises for the first time: "We are twelve brothers, the sons of one man; the youngest is this day with our father, and one is no more." Somewhat later, when they see how Simeon is being held hostage, their guilt oppresses them even more. In this scene, for the first time, their crime of long ago hangs over the brothers with somber oscillation. In this scene they see a nemesis, a retribution. They have once more to see together the same scene that they once witnessed together in wantonness, the agony of a brother—this time it cuts them to the quick:

Then they said to one another, "In truth we are guilty concerning our brother, in that we saw the distress of his soul, when he besought us and we would not listen; therefore is this distress come upon us." They did not know that Joseph understood them, for there was an interpreter between them. Then he turned away from them and wept. (Gen. 42:21, 23-24)

With unprecedented fineness, the shadow of the deceased brother glides invisibly across the scene, while the one they believed to be dead stands before them, shaken to the core. From that point on, the conversations and speeches continue alongside the dark secret, and from time to time it becomes clearer that for the brothers Joseph's shadow is the really disturbing factor complicating their present situation, after so many years. Even Joseph's reunion with them and Jacob's immigration to Egypt do not kill this dragon of guilt, for at the end, after Jacob has died, the old wound opens again, in the scene where the brothers once more surrender themselves in their torment to Joseph. Up to that point, where is the talk of God? This uncanny affair, the way the brothers' guilt trails after them, this entanglement of guilt and suffering, this nemesis could remind one of the profound pessimism of Greek tragedy, the maze of guilt in the house of Atreus or Labdacus. And yet this story is different. The sufferings that come upon the brothers are not "fate." They are initiated by Joseph; they are not even punishment, let alone reprisal; they are a test. That is what Joseph says in one of those ambiguous statements that our narrator loves: Therein will I test you (Gen. 42:16). He does not test whether they are spies. He knows that they are not. He tests whether they are the same old brothers or whether perhaps an inner change has occurred in them.

There are two stages in the test; the first occurs with Simeon, the second with Benjamin. Both deal with the same thing: Joseph isolates one brother from the rest and wants to see if they will sacrifice this one as they once sacrificed Joseph himself. Twice, with uncanny luck, he creates a situation in which they have the opportunity to sacrifice a brother. The second test especially is unbelievably severe. Whoever is not overcome with horror in the complications surrounding Joseph's cup, at the presumptuous, almost blasphemous game Joseph plays, is not fully aware of the situation. One should visualize the scene where the brothers, having found the cup in Benjamin's sack, return to Joseph in deep despair and give him with overwhelming heaviness of heart the circumstantial evidence, while Joseph addresses them coldly and severely, "What deed is this that you have done? Do you not know that such a man as I can indeed divine?" That is perhaps the most arrogant moment of all, when Joseph, before his brothers, adduces a supernatural knowledge. How closely, however, the story here touches on the still veiled, divine meaning of this entire event appears in the answer Judah makes, which again is marked by that strange ambiguity we noted above: "God has found out the guilt of your servants" (Gen. 44:16). He appears to mean the story of the cup that was found, but in fact he utters a much profounder truth, the gradual articulation of which is a theme of the whole Joseph story. The moment of that full articulation, which occurs together with Joseph's loss of self-control, takes place precisely at the end of the test. Judah's speech has made clear that the brothers will now answer for each other to the last man, and that they have passed the test.

But now we come to the final and most central question. Why did Joseph deal with his brothers in a such a way as to bring them recklessly to the verge of despair? Whence did he derive authority to do that? He had authority because he alone knew something that was hidden from all others. He alone was able to see the whole, confused event in a light in which no one else could see it. Joseph reveals that quite openly in two speeches, first in the scene of recognition and again at the end after his father's death. These two speeches contain statements that unlock the whole narrative:

So Joseph said to his brothers, "Come near to me, I pray you." . . . And he said, "I am your brother, Joseph, whom you sold into Egypt. And now do not be distressed, or angry with yourselves, because you sold me here; for God sent me before you to preserve life. . . . God sent me before you . . . to keep alive for you many survivors. So it was not you who sent me here, but God." (Gen. 45:4-8)

Here Joseph at last speaks openly of God, and here the last veil is lifted; for here, finally, is manifested what in truth is the primary subject of the whole story: God's will to turn all the chaos of human guilt to a gracious purpose. God, not the brothers, "sent" Joseph to Egypt. As one recent commentator has said, Joseph drapes the evil in a cheerful joke. But there is much more at work here than Joseph's diversionary friendliness. Joseph wants to fix everyone's attention on the supremely important fact of God's leadership that took control of all these somber events "for good." Joseph does not say, "for good," but rather, "to preserve life," "to keep alive many survivors." These sober words, that do not derive from the usual language of faith, are again typical of the penetrating worldliness of this narrator. They are to be most important to the brothers in keeping them from quarreling on their way home (Gen. 45:24). The great psychologist knows about the reactions that can erupt after such a disclosure, but they are to leave it at that.

In the second programmatic passage we touch the high point of the Joseph story. After their father's death, the brothers again feel pangs of conscience. The old man had been their protection, but now what might not Joseph do? Perhaps he had been waiting for this moment for years. At first they do not dare to see him, and that deeply disturbs Joseph. When they then appear before him with their great question, Joseph utters the most significant of all the words spoken in the story: "Fear not, for am I in the place of God? As for you, you meant evil against me; but God meant it for good" (Gen. 50:19-20).

Those words, in quite worldly language, express the most compact theology. Joseph makes two statements. In the first he defines his relationship to God, in the second his brothers' relationship to God. In the first sentence one must guard against misreading the astonished question in the sense of a very general, pious truth, i.e., of a humble statement of incompetence, as though God, not Joseph, must be the judge in this matter. For the brothers that would be cold comfort indeed if Joseph wanted simply to transfer the whole difficult matter to a higher court. Joseph's meaning is much more than that. He means to say that here, in the miraculous course of the whole affair, God himself has spoken. He has incorporated the evil into his saving activity and therewith expressed a justification. If Joseph were now to condemn his brothers, he would be making a judgment on his own that would stand alongside what God had already expressed in the events themselves, and in doing that he would be putting himself "in the place of God."

The second statement is closely connected with Joseph's word at his self-revelation to his brothers, except that it emphasizes the enigmatic interaction of God's providence and man's action even more strongly. Even at the point where no man could accept more, God had all the threads in his hand. That is asserted, however, not expounded; the how of this interaction remains a mystery. Thus the words, "You meant" and "God meant" stubbornly contradict each other. The ancient teachers of wisdom knew this. "A man's mind plans his way, but the Lord directs his steps" (Prov. 16:9). "A man's steps are ordered by the Lord; how then can man understand his way?" (Prov. 20:24). This astonishment, this "how can man understand his way?" pervades the entire Joseph story, in spite of that story's sober worldliness.

Previously we said that earlier Israel had seen God's activity in sacred wars, connected with sacred institutions, with cults, the holy ark, or the charisma of men of God who suddenly appeared on the scene. Now, however, the royal era had come bringing its great intellectual upheaval. It did not dispute what had been believed in an earlier period. What fascinated its sages, however, was something different, something new. It was the hidden rule of God, the unseen rule that took hold of everything, bending the schemings of the human heart to its purpose without restraining them.

Strange change in our conclusion! At the beginning we spoke of the permeation and predominance of what is human in the Joseph story and of the way God is mentioned only peripherally. If, now, one takes seriously Joseph's statement about God's universal rule, then man's activity is reduced to virtual irrelevance in the face of such all-sufficiency of the divine ruler. And this is indeed a problem. I would not want to hide the fact that this extremely comforting word of Joseph's, precisely in its harsh separation between divine and human action, poses from the start a theological problem; for it relegates God's action to radical secrecy, distance, and unrecognizableness. So long as the charismatic interpreter was present, as in the Joseph story, there was no danger. But Joseph's word nevertheless contains a radical cognition of faith; and what happened when one was left alone with this knowledge appears for us in the book of Ecclesiastes, in which the question, "How can a man understand his way?" has taken on an undercurrent of doubt. There we read that a man cannot comprehend God's work (or God's rule) from beginning to end (3:11).

> Then I saw all the work of God, that man cannot find out the work that is done under the sun. However much man may toil in seeking, he will not find it out; even though a wise man claims to know, he cannot find it out. (Eccles. 8:17)

> As you do not know how the spirit comes to the bones in the womb of a woman with child, so you do not know the work of God who makes everything. (Eccles. 11:5)

Precisely a mental attitude like that of post-Solomonic wisdom, which has become aware of its rational powers and organizational opportunities and has ventured so close to the limits of the human realm, is reticent with respect to the ultimate ground of the world. There exists, I believe, a very close connection between that almost hybrid apprehension and traversal and interpretation of the world on the one hand, and on the other, that knowledge about the absolute limit that exists for human discovery, where it concerns the divine ground of the world. The scepticism of the preacher in Ecclesiastes is rooted in the distant past!

But we return to the Joseph story. The fact that in the Joseph story a person's act, whether good or bad, is reduced almost to irrelevance by the superior might of God's control, does not mean that the question of the brothers' guilt is minimized. We are, of course, fascinated first of all with Joseph's wonderful composure regarding his brothers' guilt, with the absence of every moral passion. Nowhere is there zeal to define the guilt more precisely or any enthusiasm to reveal it. Instead, the narrative gives a clear answer to the question of guilt. It is indeed noteworthy that the brothers in the end, when they beg Joseph's forgiveness, mention the faith they share with him. " 'Forgive, I pray you, the transgression of your brothers and their sin, because they did evil to you.' And now, we pray you, forgive the transgression of the servants of the God of your father" (Gen. 50:17).

Forgiveness among men is not purely an inter-personal affair; it extends in every instance deeply into the relationship of a man to God. Joseph's answer to his brothers' request is his statement that he can under no circumstances allow another verdict to fall in the place of God's. God incorporated this shadowed terrain of human passions into his saving rule. Indeed he allowed the brothers themselves to receive his "salvation," as a few of those "many survivors." That permission contains his forgiveness. But we should once more discover the noteworthy, worldly character of his narrative in the almost indirect way all of this is expressed, the way forgiveness is here mentioned—in the avoidance of all traditional, pious, or cultural formulas and words. Without question, the Joseph story was for its time a modern story, and Joseph was a modern man.

3

THE STORY ABOUT BALAAM

(Lecture on South German radio in the series "Faith and Life," Bible stories, December 1953.)

Why is ancient Israel's path through history so strange, so different from that of other peoples? Why were the dangers to which she was exposed more deadly, the consolations and fulfillments she found in history more profound and splendid? The Old Testament answers, it was because Israel met the living God in her history and because God granted her again and again men who knew how to interpret these encounters fully.

This story (Numbers 22–24) concerns itself with ancient lore. Israel, in her desert wandering, has come quite near the promised land, when she is met by the Moabite king, Balak. He does not come, as one expects him to do, with an armed host or with any external force, but rather with a lone man more dangerous than an entire army: namely, Balaam the sorcerer. "Come now, curse this people for me, since they are too mighty for me." We enlightened, urbanized westerners scarcely know any more what a curse is. A curse is infinitely more than an evil word or wicked slander. The ancients believed that one who cursed brought on something thoroughly evil, reached beyond the realm of prominent reality, and enticed profoundly abysmal, destructive forces. Not everyone could do that. But every nation knew such people with mysterious access to this realm of thoroughly evil powers, even with uncanny powers of command over them. Such a man, known and feared far and near, was Balaam. And Balaam had started out immediately at Balak's request. Powers like that are available in the world for hire! But the angel of the Lord met the unsuspecting traveler with drawn sword. Three times the angel barred the way, and the ass saw the angel before its rider and renowned sorcerer did. When one is in league with the demonic powers, even a beast apparently has a better scent for God's word and revelation! When Balaam finally recognized the angel of the Lord, he did what everyone expects he would do, he volunteered to go back home!

But now comes the surprise: he is *not* to return, but rather to speak faithfully the word that will be given to him. One could call that the "tense moment" of the story. Every reader followed the course of events with apprehension, for Balaam's intent was indeed diabolical, and now God does *not* bar his way but lets him go on. How will it turn out? To be sure, God directs history and fortune in such a way that he does not continually restrain people from doing what they planned. He lets them act, and they do apparently just what they planned to do, discovering in the process that they have been God's instrument to do his will.

Balaam has arrived and goes straight to his tasks. He is led to a hill from which he can see Israel—but only the nearest part—encamped in the valley. He makes all the preparations for his solemn ceremony of cursing. Seven altars were constructed; offerings were made; Balaam changed the place from which he would speak several times, according to the custom of those who practice such magical rites. These details of sorcery are described quite realistically, and the effect of the oracles that Balaam utters is thus even more impressive: "How can I curse whom God has not cursed? How can I denounce whom the Lord has not denounced?"

With this first pronouncement the story has reached its climax. Here the amazing inner side of the sinister affair begins to appear: Balaam cannot curse Israel at all. Where God has pronounced a blessing, there the most vehement curse encounters a frontier. "For from the top of the mountains I see him, from the hills I behold him; lo, a people dwelling alone, and not reckoning itself among the nations!" The peace enjoyed unconsciously by Israel as it camps in the valley is particularly beautiful in the face of the battle that has broken out completely beyond the realm of earthly powers. The context of forces that this story presents is indeed very strange. The earthly opponents are completely inactive. The Moabites watch Balaam, and Israel camps unsuspecting in the valley. At work are the powers above the earthly contest: here Balaam mobilizing demonic powers, and here God, the Lord. The outcome of this struggle does not depend on men, but occurs at a higher level. The Reformers would have called it a contest between God and the Devil.

And Balaam has to keep on speaking blessings: "How fair are your tents, O Jacob, your encampments, O Israel! Like valleys that stretch afar, like gardens beside a river, like aloes that the Lord has planted, like cedar trees beside the waters. Water shall flow from his buckets, and his seed shall be in many waters!" One can see how the seer's horizon expands with each utterance. The charisma grows once Balaam begins to resign himself to God's will. And now—a wonderful detail!—he can see all Israel, God's people encamped by tribes.

Balak is infuriated when he hears these unexpected oracles of blessing; he strikes his hands together over his head and wants to drive Balaam away. Balaam starts to go, but as he turns to leave he pronounces a final oracle. In this oracle we sense remotely something about the external origin of a prophecy, about the arduous concentration and the suppression of every personal feeling in the breast: "The oracle of Balaam the son of Beor, the oracle of the man whose eye is opened, the oracle of him who hears the words of God, and knows the knowledge of the Most High, who sees the vision of the Almighty, falling down, but having his eyes uncovered." And now the outlines of what he sees begin to become clearer. "I see him, but not now; I behold him, but not nigh: a star shall come forth out of Jacob, and a scepter shall rise out of Israel." That is the Messiah, and with that Balaam has touched on the last thing. After this high point the story ends abruptly. Balak leaves Israel alone, and Balaam returns to his home.

This story is not, of course, a pointless narrative. It too is a confession: God is for his people. Their defense is not found in men and is not dependent at all on the alignments of worldly powers. Even more, the most sinister plots against God's people must work for their good. Even a Balaam has to bless! My friends, how often have Christians been blessed by Balaam! This Old Testament story thus anticipates the New Testament statement, that all things work together for good to those who love God.

4

JUDGES 12:5-7

(First published in Men of the Evangelical Church in Germany. *A volume honoring Kurt Scharf on his sixtieth birthday. Lettner Verlag, Berlin-Stuttgart, 1962, pp. 194-95.)*

And the Gileadites took the fords of the Jordan against the Ephraimites. And when any of the fugitives of Ephraim said, "Let me go over," the men of Gilead said to him, "Are you an Ephraimite?" When he said, "No," they said to him, "then say Shibboleth," and he said, "Sibboleth," for he could not pronounce it right; then they seized him and slew him at the fords of the Jordan. And there fell at that time forty-two thousand of the Ephraimites. Jephthah judged Israel six years.

These verses belong to a longer narrative that tells about Jephthah's wars against the Ammonites, but also about the internal quarrels that broke out among the Israelite tribes themselves, once the external threat had been removed. These quarrels led to antagonism between the western and eastern tribes so that the Jordan river became the hostile boundary between the brothers on the east and those on the west. Something can be said to clarify the rivalries and their basis, for the tradition is ancient and reliable. But it cannot be asserted that this sequel, in which tribal rivals win the upper hand, has much historical importance. One thing, however, must be designated as important: the uncompromising matter-of-factness with which the narrator presents the events, and only the events, a matter-of-factness that we know in many passages from the Old Testament. The narrator neither praises nor blames; he draws no conclusions and presents no consequences or lessons. He is concerned only with the event as such. Whoever knows something about how fast a historical event is delivered up to some interpretation or other in a people's memory, or is taken over by some political or religious ideology, that person must admit that the strict objectivity of this report, its respect for the value of history, is something rare in popular literature. Here, harshly and apparently without feeling, we are given a slice, a very small slice, of ancient history. In those days the people of God treated each other that way, with that kind of simplicity they dispatched those who differed from themselves: one word decided the matter! It is significant enough that the meaning of that word, "shibboleth," in this context is not at all clear. (Does it mean "ear"?) It does not matter. We are not dealing with a confession of some kind, the content of which was decisive, but simply with a completely empty word on which life and death were made to depend. (The modern reader will scarcely control himself. He does what the ancient narrator did not allow himself to do: he passes judgment upon the event as being repulsive and as vulgar as possible.)

The ancient reader had reservations about how the Jordan river could have been the boundary between Israel and Israel. The concluding verse to the whole narrative, verse 7, is very strange: "Jephthah judged Israel." Israel? One who reads the story cannot be deceived about the regional boundaries of Jephthah's sphere of influence. How, then, can one say that he judged "Israel"? The statement, Old Testament scholars agree, comes not from our storyteller, who is to be dated early; it belongs, rather, to the deuteronomistic framework of events. It comes from a theological workshop where one was no longer so well-informed about many historical details, but where, with respect to the whole history of God's people, a few decisive new insights prevailed. Here then, finally, is interpretation: This wretched multitude over which God placed the charismatic, Jephthah, was indeed "Israel"! This people, consuming itself in internal quarrels, among whom someone made a difference in dialects the criterion for life and death, was indeed God's people, Israel, for whom God intended peace, not harm.

5

THE STORY ABOUT SAMSON

(Lecture on South German radio in the series, "Faith and Life," Bible stories, December 1953.)

"And the house fell upon the lords and upon all the people that were in it. So the dead whom he slew at his death were more than those whom he had slain during his life." With this somber and very melancholy statement the story about Samson comes to an end. (See Judges 13–16.)

Who was this Samson? We think of a gigantic, long-haired, powerful man, who murders people, tears apart lions, overturns houses, and performs astonishing exploits that impress us much less than they make us smile a little because they appear unseemly. But this image that has come down to us, for which Christian instruction must bear some blame, is very incomplete and superficial. The ancient biblical narrator wants to show us a great deal more.

First of all, no reader of these ancient stories is excused from visualizing the historical conditions of that time. About 1200 B.C. the Israelite tribes were living primarily in the hill country, because the large Palestinian plain to the west was occupied by the Canaanites and Philistines. The tribe living closest to the Philistines was the tribe of Dan on the western slope of the Judaean hill country, and it lived, therefore, in constant communication with the Philistines. In such local friction, life and death were regularly at stake. That was an extremely harsh, rough time, a kind of early Middle Ages, youthfully exuberant, bursting with strength, not sorry for itself, not humane; and Samson was like that. The stories about him are often quite gross, and we ought not to teach them from the standpoint of a modern humaneness. All peoples have experienced rough times like those in their cultural development.

But why does the Bible mention this mighty man who played so many nasty tricks on the Philistines? This Samson, even before his birth, was destined to belong to God in a special way. More than others, he was to be an instrument in God's hand, to be available to God. The ancient Israelites called such people of God Nazirites. Nazirites refrained from drinking wine, were not permitted to cut their hair, and lived, therefore, in a way that would arouse their more thoughtless contemporaries. Samson's life thus had an important history with respect to God. The narrative, in which the angel of God appeared to Samson's parents, has become memorable for many because of a painting by Rembrandt.

One who has looked at the devout picture of Samson's call in the 13th chapter of Judges is greatly surprised with the way the narrator thereafter stirs up a whirl of quite secular stories. Samson pursues the women and has dangerous and often truly comic adventures. There is the story of the banquet with the Philistines. Samson sits down to eat with men who wish him no good. Their gathering is not at all cordial. They dine and tell jokes, but the atmosphere is tense. Still, the arrogant rivalry is restricted to the intellectual. The men compete shrewdly by telling clever riddles, a popular game in those days: "What is sweeter than honey, what is stronger than a lion? Love!" But this rivalry ends in blood. Later Samson drives foxes with firebrands on their tails through the wheat fields of the Philistines; another time he spends nights in Gaza with a prostitute. That time the Philistines believed they had him, for the city gates were closed for the night. But Samson, after a night of love, at midnight pulled up the city gates with their posts and bar and carried them away many kilometers to the top of a hill at Hebron. But then he fell in love with Delilah, and she was his undoing. From then on his decline was swift, for, as the narrator tells us, "the Lord had left him." We see him, the invincible one, lying defenseless on the bosom of a cunning woman—that too is a scene that has charmed countless artists. And finally Samson is delivered by his own people, for whom also he had become sinister, to his deadly enemies. He is blinded and forced to grind at the mill in prison. But at a great feast he, the defeated one, was brought out to amuse the crowd. He was placed in the middle of the hall between two pillars that supported the palace roof; there he was to entertain the multitude. But in a final surge of strength he pulled down the pillars, burying himself and the celebrating crowd under the ruins.

What does all that mean? How can we find our way in these stories, in which right and wrong are so hopelessly intertwined? Was it right for Samson to drive the foxes into the wheat fields? Was it right for his own countrymen to have delivered him to the Philistines? Was it right? Surely we could continue a long time with questions. But the key lies elsewhere. Samson had been unusually gifted by God. Not only his physical strength, but especially his wit and readiness for battle are amazing. With these great gifts went a simplicity and guilelessness that make him seem to us like a child with whom one cannot be seriously angry. And at the end he falls victim to those who were not so strong and not so witty, but all the more underhanded. Should we not see in him a tragic figure? When we talk about the tragic, we think of impersonal fate. Here we have something completely different. Samson had a divine commission, and for that commission he was granted divine gifts. The New Testament calls that endowment for doing God's will charisma. But what did Samson do with it? His life reveals a continuous alternation between demonstrations of strength and of humiliating weakness. His divine strength is wasted again and again on ineffectual, practical jokes. He plays with his charisma and does not use it in obedience.

Thus the stories of Samson paint a picture of squandered, God-given strength; it was spent in pulling things down. The stories show a deplorable defect in the struggle between eros and charisma. Samson accomplishes nothing, and he perishes at last in the chaos that he has spread about him. "So the dead whom he slew at his death were more than those whom he had slain during his life."

6

NAAMAN:
A CRITICAL RETELLING

(First published in Medicus Viator. "Questions and Thoughts" *suggested by the career of Richard Siebeck. A volume given by his friends and students on the occasion of his seventy-fifth birthday. J. C. B. Mohr (Paul Siebeck), Tübingen, and George Thieme, Stuttgart, 1959, pp. 297-305.)*

Anyone who interprets an ancient, literary document like a story has a great advantage if he can define the sociological milieu out of which it arose and for which it was also presumably intended. For Old Testament literature this good fortune seldom occurs, but for the stories that cluster about the prophet Elisha (II Kings 2–13:21) one can say that it does.

These stories arose at about the same time and were only much later incorporated into the comprehensive historical work that is primarily First and Second Kings. The stories reveal a social milieu, one could almost say they make palpable the atmosphere of a group of men in Israel of the ninth century B.C. To be sure, they deal with a very strange stratum of the society in Israel at that time. There was—and the Dead Sea Scrolls suggest that there always were—in Israel, in addition to the classes of courtiers, priests, and peasants of the kingdom, a group of religious men that can be included only with difficulty in the usual social categories. The men of that group lived in the vicinity of shrines as though in individual congregations; they listened to the doctrinal lectures of their prophetic masters. For the rest, they lived in extreme poverty and almost give the impression of being outside the class structure. The people, however, seem to have revered them. We do not know what those prophets spoke about in their lectures, but from all the stories about their leader and master, the prophet Elisha, we feel a breath of their spirit. We select one of these stories here, namely, the one about the Aramaean Naaman's encounter with the prophet Elisha and what went on between these two men at that time (II Kings 5).

This Naaman (ná-ə-man) was a man of very high rank. He was the generalissimo of the Aramaeans; and he was, as the narrator emphasizes, an extraordinarily honest man. Unusual as it was to picture as a partner to the prophet an Aramaean—who was one of the most influential men among these deadly enemies of Israel, a man indeed who was a pagan, whom the narrator describes from the first sentence forward with obvious respect—it is even more strange for this beginning to be intensified with the remark that God had given victory to Syria because of this excellent Naaman. The remark is brief, but in ancient Israel no one would have missed it. Naaman was, then, someone for whose sake God had blessed Israel's enemies. And this man, to conclude the setting for the story, was a leper.

The first instrument God offered for saving this man was a little Israelite girl, who had fallen into the hands of the Aramaeans as a captive of war and then had arrived in Naaman's house. She spoke to her mistress about the prophet in Israel who would surely heal her ailing lord if he would go to him. Her speech was quite simple, and the narrator uses it to prepare for a contrast; for things thereafter did not proceed so simply. At all events the narrator has strongly emphasized the hiddenness of God's ways and the plainness of his means. The road which men designated for this affair to follow contrasts in a most curious manner with God's gentle means.

Naaman spoke with his king, and the latter sent him to Samaria with royal presents and a letter of safe-conduct.

This letter, only the outline of which is given, following ancient literary custom, is imperious and blunt: The king of Israel is to cure this Naaman of leprosy. One can see that the Aramaean king has not comprehended the matter at all. He thinks that if such art of healing is practiced in Israel, the king, more than any other person, must have charge of it. Whether he was thinking of special, sacred, cultic functions, which in the ancient orient were reserved for the king alone, cannot be learned from the text. In any event, the Aramaean could not imagine that in Israel divine gifts of grace were granted quite apart from the hierarchy of human social rank.

The Israelite king was outraged. It speaks well of him that he could not comprehend this unreasonable demand at all. Does he think I am a God? No, he is looking for trouble! According to Israel's faith God alone was competent for all healing. Israel knew about medicines and therapy, but it took zealous care to see that God's glory not be compromised. Wherever there was sickness and healing, there was in Israel also a *status confessionis*; and the king at once had reacted in this characteristic way.

But Naaman's affair was now finally bungled; it had been maneuvered into the realm of politics, into an atmosphere of mistrust and insinuations, in which good can no longer flourish. The way God had prepared now seemed hopelessly blocked. The course of events that led to this first failure is almost grotesque. In the continuation of the story the reader cannot escape seeing how the events are occasionally presented in their comic aspects too.

Elisha, whom the narrative makes at home in Samaria, has meanwhile heard of the events at the court and has sent a message to the king that he should let the stranger come to him. From here on the story moves swiftly to its first climax. Naaman came "with his horses and chariots," i.e., with his entire retinue, to what was surely the very modest dwelling of the man of God. And Elisha did not even give him a glance; he merely sent a young man with the advice that Naaman should dip himself seven times in the Jordan river, and he would be healed.

One can comprehend the full affront of this scene when one considers that the Jordan and its water enjoyed no trace of sacred value in ancient Israel. Keeping in mind everything we know about the religious conceptions of this time, we cannot assume that there existed anywhere anything like a sacramental rite of baptism. But we do not need this reflection, for the narrator himself argues, by the contrast he creates, against any sacred magic. If Elisha intended to offend the Aramaean, he succeeded. Naaman is enraged and expresses openly how everything he had thought and hoped would happen did not. He had first of all assumed that Elisha would at least come out; then he had expected a solemn, magic procedure with a call on God's name and mysterious gestures. In his disappointment over what had not occurred he thinks of his home and of what, as he now thinks he can see, he had left behind. "Are not the waters of Damascus better than all the waters of Israel?" The abundant waters of Damascus were considered a marvel by the peoples of antiquity, and later they were still an inexhausted object of Arabic poetry. What Naaman meant with his reflection has indeed far-reaching importance. We can paraphrase it perhaps as follows: Damascus too has myth and magical rites, which are perhaps actually better than those of Israel. One who seeks them should not journey to Israel and her prophets. What Naaman does not know at the time is that Elisha wanted to disabuse him completely of this search for a miracle, this lust for cloudy vapor and magical twilight. He did not come out himself, because he wanted to dissociate himself from the event of healing. Here certainly one myth should not be outbid by another. For that reason Elisha had simply demanded the man's obedience. Thus for a second time everything would have been nearly ruined if simple men had not intervened. Men in the general's company, not so encircled by the walls of their pride, finally brought the sick man to accept the prophet's advice by their simple words; and Naaman was miraculously healed.

If our narrative were to be designated as a "miracle story," of the kind known in countless variations in ancient and recent times, it could now end with a confession of gratitude to be sure on the part of the healed man. The remarkable element of our story, however, is that its climax comes after Naaman's healing, that it deals with problems that grow out of that event. There is no doubt that the story has two climactic points: Naaman's encounter with Elisha, and his conversation with Elisha at the end. The healing forms a bridge over the depression between both high points.

Naaman has returned full of gratitude to Elisha and has tried, in the exuberance of his feelings, to force expensive gifts upon him. When he encounters strict refusal, his own recent faith in the God who has helped him becomes a problem—the motivation is psychologically convincing—in the presence of such strength of devotion and so uncompromising a totality of service as that of Elisha. He has to ask the prophet two questions. First he asks for a load of Israelite soil, as much as two mules can carry, to take with him to Damascus so that he will be able to worship God there correctly, "for henceforth your servant will not offer burnt offering or sacrifice to any god but the Lord." That was a very strange request, certainly also in the narrator's mind. Notwithstanding, it is doubtful that recent interpreters are right in seeing in that request proof of how deeply this man was mired in his heathenism. Can a load of earth help his faith? One can see, we are told, that he thinks very childishly of God as being limited to the land of Palestine. But that is inconsistent with his solemn confession that there is no God in all the earth except in Israel, which does not mean that the competence of this God does not extend beyond the borders of Israel. Still, this awareness does not restrain him from asking for the load of earth. The mistake interpreters persist in making stems from the unspoken, philosophical premise that

Israel divided the world into material and spiritual parts and that religion deals only with the spiritual, which can have only an inward character. Israel believed, however, that God by his self-revelation laid claim to all mankind and the whole world, spiritual and material, internal and spatially objective, and that God will not be satisfied simply with man's inner nature. (Moreover, one should bear in mind that the story does give inner feelings their due insofar as it introduces very delicate questions of the kind that could have arisen only in this particular person.) Admittedly, the ancient Israelite reading this request for a load of earth would also have found it rather strange simply because one ordinarily left the earth of the promised land where it was. But he would not have marveled at all over Naaman's presumed inability to recognize the spiritual truth. Rather he would have been moved by the way in which a new-found faith here expresses anxiety about remaining alive out in the heathen world and asks for the Palestinian soil as a temporary expedient, an insulating layer, so to speak, from on-rushing heathendom. Indeed, it would not be difficult to show how Christendom has made use of a load of holy ground—in the particular style of its hymns, its language, its buildings, its symbols, and its liturgical movements—against the profane world. In the theological dialogue between biblical faith and the Greek spirit, which must in the west be continually conducted afresh, that mule-load of earth has a role to play.

But the second request is much more risky. Naaman's high position will make it unavoidable that, at certain celebrations of the official, state religion in Damascus, he should accompany his king into the temple of the imperial Aramaean god. The ceremony demanded that the king (when he prostrated himself?) "be supported" by his paladin, and Naaman would not be able in the future to escape that. There can be no doubt that the Israelite reader had to regard this request as highly questionable. Naaman too, however, felt the unusual quality of his request; for he knew that he had to request God's "pardon." He seems to have known what the first commandment says about that, and the way he poses his question lets one understand that he had indeed comprehended God's will in this matter. On the other hand, he also knows that when he returns to the heathendom of his home, he will be unable to separate himself from it. Will that be the end of his new-found faith? That is the question. We might formulate it this way: Naaman asks if the command of God will kill him when he goes out there. The sharpness of the conflict that he anticipates will here too become clear only when one comprehends that in Naaman's question a humanity is speaking that does not know about the modern escape, namely the retreat from the world into the inwardness of the heart, where the external circumstances of worship are unimportant.

In these two questions the narrator has created a marvelous climax for the story. With a few statements he has shown how an entire horizon of new problems has opened up with the healing of this man. Everything waits tensely for the prophet's word. His answer, "Go in peace," is almost bewilderingly brief. Is it really an answer? As a matter of fact, earlier interpreters found it difficult that the prophet, especially in the second case, seems to concede something he had no business conceding. There are late Jewish texts that have Elisha answering at great length: he refers Naaman to the temple in Jerusalem as the only legitimate place for sacrifice. Now this expansion of the original text is obvious, but a glance at the more recent commentaries shows that the meaning of Elisha's answer is not always understood clearly and unambiguously at all. Theologically critical interpreters think of the answer as being more or less self-evident, as though Naaman's requests were such that Elisha could not refuse them, as one commentator suggests. Not at all! Anyone who cannot see that Naaman's questions are each directed at utmost extremes, to yield to which involved great risk, does not comprehend Elisha's answer. It is brief as possible and leaves much open, but in its roominess and theological precision it is the product of genuine prophetic intuition. It is theologically precise in invoking no law against the man who is setting out for a very threatened existence; i.e., it is in no way casuistic. Elisha dismisses the man. Indeed, one has the impression that he thrusts him out into the uncertainties of his future life without providing for him any moral or religiously detailed guidance at all. He leaves him completely to his new faith, or better, to God's hand which has sought and found him. When one considers how difficult Elisha made things for Naaman at the beginning, how he humiliated him, one must be surprised at the almost presumptuous freedom into which he now directs him. If we look back once more at Naaman, as he waits eagerly for the answer to his questions, we have to recall two statements about Jesus that seem to be presaged in Elisha's answer: "Jesus looking upon him loved him!" and "I have not found such faith in all Israel."

The story is not quite finished. It tells how Gehazi, Elisha's young servant, hastened after the departing Naaman because he could not get over the fact that his master had accepted none of all the costly gifts Naaman had offered. With a bald lie he acquired a good share of them for himself, not difficult to be sure, because the unsuspecting Naaman gladly seized the opportunity to attest his gratitude once again. The picture of that poor devil who now like a lord can let his servants precede him bearing the treasures, but who at the last chain of hills must take the treasures from their hands and put them under cover for safe-keeping, bespeaks a highly amusing situation. But Elisha in spirit has perceived everything, and Gehazi is punished with leprosy. This end to the story has no real independence; it is only the unedifying counterpart to the story of Naaman. It points however, to something very bitter: how well things went for the heathen king, and how desperate the failure in the prophet's own house!

In conclusion, we ask again about the story's purpose.

It is certainly not purposeless, i.e., it is not told purely for joy in the event and its telling. What then about its didactic intent? We have to say that its teaching is only slight and suppressed. In this story the listener or reader is called upon to pay careful attention, because otherwise he will not apprehend the moral at all. This brings us back to the beginning of our discussion, to the indigent associations of the prophets. It is moving to see the theological problems with which the men of these circles occupied theselves. One cannot call this a "popular" story, as is often done. What follows is the English translation.

Naaman, commander of the army of the king of Syria, was a great man with his master and in high favor, because by him the Lord had given victory to Syria. He was a mighty man of valor, but he was a leper. Now the Syrians on one of their raids had carried off a little maid from the land of Israel, and she waited on Naaman's wife. She said to her mistress, "Would that my lord were with the prophet who is in Samaria! He would cure him of his leprosy." So Naaman went in and told his lord, "Thus and so spoke the maiden from the land of Israel." And the king of Syria said, "Go now, and I will send a letter to the king of Israel."

So he went, taking with him ten talents of silver, six thousand shekels of gold, and ten festal garments. And he brought the letter to the king of Israel, which read, "When this letter reaches you, know that I have sent to you Naaman my servant, that you may cure him of his leprosy." And when the king of Israel read the letter, he rent his clothes and said, "Am I God, to kill and to make alive, that this man sends word to me to cure a man of his leprosy? Only consider, and see how he is seeking a quarrel with me."

But when Elisha the man of God heard that the king of Israel had rent his clothes, he sent to the king, saying, "Why have you rent your clothes? Let him come now to me, that he may know that there is a prophet in Israel." So Naaman came with his horses and chariots, and halted at the door of Elisha's house. And Elisha sent a messenger to him, saying, "Go and wash in the Jordan seven times, and your flesh shall be restored, and you shall be clean." But Naaman was angry, and went away, saying, "Behold, I thought that he would surely come out to me, and stand,

and call on the name of the Lord his God, and wave his hand over the place, and cure the leper. Are not Abana and Pharpar, the rivers of Damascus, better than all the waters of Israel? Could I not wash in them, and be clean?" So he turned and went away in a rage. But his servants came near and said to him, "My father, if the prophet had commanded you to do some great thing, would you not have done it? How much rather, then, when he says to you, 'Wash, and be clean?' " So he went down and dipped himself seven times in the Jordan, according to the word of the man of God; and his flesh was restored like the flesh of a little child, and he was clean.

Then he returned to the man of God, he and all his company, and he came and stood before him; and he said, "Behold, I know that there is no God in all the earth but in Israel; so accept now a present from your servant." But he said, "As the Lord lives, whom I serve, I will receive none." And he urged him to take it, but he refused. Then Naaman said, "If not, I pray you, let there be given to your servant two mules' burden of earth; for henceforth your servant will not offer burnt offering or sacrifice to any god but the Lord. In this matter may the Lord pardon your servant: when my master goes into the house of Rimmon to worship there, leaning on my arm, and I bow myself in the house of Rimmon, when I bow myself in the house of Rimmon, the Lord pardon your servant in this matter." He said to him, "Go in peace."

But when Naaman had gone from him a short distance, Gehazi, the servant of Elisha the man of God, said, "See, my master has spared this Naaman the Syrian, in not accepting from his hand what he brought. As the Lord lives, I will run after him, and get something from him." So Gehazi followed Naaman. And when Naaman saw some one running after him, he alighted from the chariot to meet him, and said, "Is all well?" And he said, "All is well. My master has sent me to say, 'There have just now come to me from the hill country of Ephraim two young men of the sons of the prophets; pray, give them a talent of silver and two festal garments.' " And Naaman said, "Be pleased to accept two talents." And he urged him, and tied up two talents of silver in two bags, with two festal garments, and laid them upon two of his servants; and they carried them before Gehazi. And when he came to the hill, he took them from their hand, and put them in the house; and he sent the men away, and they departed. He went in, and stood before his master, and Elisha said to him, "Where have you been, Gehazi?" And he said, "Your servant went nowhere." But he said to him, "Did I not go with you in spirit when the man turned from his chariot to meet you? Was it a time to accept money and garments, olive orchards and vineyards, sheep and oxen, menservants and maidservants? Therefore the leprosy of Naaman shall cleave to you, and to your descendants for ever." So he went out from his presence a leper, as white as snow. (II Kings 5)

God acts out of love. He desires the sacrifice of the heart - not all the burnt offerings of the world.

Acts 8:9-24

7

THE PROPHET JONAH

(First published by Laetare-Verlag, Nürnberg, 1950.)

When one studies the history of interpretation of the book of Jonah, from that of the early church through that of the Reformation and the modern era, one is left with the depressing thought that Christendom has not often, perhaps, been really pleased with its possession of this wonderful document.[1] The reason it has not, strangely, is that the church all too often believed itself to be in the painful position of having to justify God in some way or other. Luther expressed himself with some feeling on the subject: "By God, what a marvelous work it is! Who can sufficiently comprehend that a person should live three days and three nights in a fish in the midst of the sea, alone, without light, without food, and come out alive? That was indeed a rare cruise. Who would believe it and not think it a cock-and-bull story, if it were not in the Bible?"[2] Even here a note of perplexity is unmistakable. And that widely respected professor of theology in 18th century Goettingen, who explained with great scientific precision that it was not a fish at all but rather a ship called "The Great Fish" that took Jonah aboard, that

---

[1]P. Friedrichsen, *Kritische Uebersicht der verschiedenen Ansichten von dem Buche Jonas,* 2. Aufl. 1841. Frz. Delitzsch, "Etwas ueber das Buch Jona und einige neue Auslegungen desselben." *Zeitschr. f.d. gesammte luth. Theologie und Kirche* 1840, 112 ff.

[2]M. Luther, *Der Prophet Jona ausgel.* (1526), Weimarana Bd. 19, 210.

learned man is only a symptom of the general lack of comprehension.

We begin with the very simple fact that the little book is a *story,* which means that only the person who is open and ready to hear a story will comprehend it. Perhaps our understanding of the Old Testament would be better if we were accustomed more often to theologize the art of simple telling and listening to stories.

I

In the kingdom of Israel, the so-called northern kingdom, there lived in the days of King Jeroboam II (II Kings 14:25) a man of God, one of those prophets through whom God expressed in history his will and his plans. One day there came to this man Jonah from God the command that he should go to Nineveh, the capital of the Assyrian empire (and of Israel's great enemy) to preach "against it." At this point the storyteller may well have paused, for his listeners had to recover from their shock at this terribly unreasonable demand that was made of Jonah. How, then, is Jonah prepared for such a task? Apparently he has only a word from God, and with that he is sent quite on his own into the great city! Of course the listener is not surprised to learn that Jonah doesn't want to go! For the moment nothing further is said about the reason for his disobedience. Does he fear for his life? Does he not trust the word of God to be effective in the great city? Much later it will become clear that Jonah fled from God for quite a different reason. This flight was no precipitate, mindless affair at all; rather the decision must have been made in cold blood, so to speak. For instead of setting off for the northeast, Jonah went to the southwest and boarded a ship in Joppa to go to Tarshish in southwestern Spain, i.e., to the outer limits of the ancient world. Imagine what it must have cost Jonah in material goods and chattel to flee from the sight of Israel's God.

When they were underway at sea, however, a furious storm broke forth, and the ship was in extreme peril.

Everyone can easily imagine what was going on aboard that small ship. But since in ancient times no one considered such misfortunes to be simply the result of natural causes, not only were all necessary gestures executed, men also prayed fervently. (The words "each cried to his god" says all that is needed about the international composition of the ship's occupants.) Jonah, of course, could not pray with them. What should he pray? So he went down to his cabin, lay down, and went to sleep.

This sleep is Jonah's first incomprehensible act. He was the only one aboard who knew what had happened and what connection it had with this peril! Luther too was indignant about Jonah's sleep: "There he lies, snoring in his sins; he neither hears nor feels what God's anger is doing or intending with him." (What a difference from Paul's sleep aboard ship in the New Testament!) But Jonah's remorseless impenitence was noticed. The people went below to him and took him to task; and therewith, in the rolling ship, began an extraordinary, religious conversation, while outside the deadly waves were pounding the ship. The passengers and crew had quickly made a connection between their peril and someone's guilt. Even more, they had apparently felt instinctively that something was wrong in the religious life of their strange fellow-passenger. Jonah, indeed, had to confess; for when faced with those ultimate questions the ancients could neither remain silent nor give false answer. But the way Jonah pathetically recited his confession in this situation was fearful: "I am a Hebrew; and I fear the Lord, the God of heaven, who made the sea and the dry land."

Even in this situation he savors the honor and pride of being a messenger of this almighty God! But now the matter has become very difficult for the ship's company. It was clear to them that God's anger was directed against Jonah alone, but it was still a delicate matter for them to lay violent hands on the servant of so mighty a God. In this conflict Jonah himself, curiously, came to their aid. He advised them to throw him into the sea. So great was his obstinacy that he would rather die than undertake

God's commission. It is a fine testimony to the men that they did not at first perceive that and instead tried once more to battle the storm. But soon they decided to abandon Jonah, and thereupon the storm ceased. The proceeding affected them profoundly, and they offered a sacrifice—later apparently, when they were on land—to the God of this prophet. Now, then, one of God's ways has reached its goal, for the unbelieving ship's company have converted to belief in and worship of the one living God. In fact, Jonah had actually helped them to do so. But by what a circuitous route of disobedience and obstinacy! Still, one must consider him an instrument of God for the well-being of men.

Jonah, however, did not drown. A great sea monster swallowed him, and Jonah lived for three days and three nights in its body. The questions about the fish and the miracle that have troubled Christians for nearly two thousand years apparently did not concern our storyteller at all. For him the fish was simply a sign that God fulfills his purposes even in dimensions that are fearful and chaotic. The storyteller also lets us marvel that now Jonah too prays.

When the fish had spat Jonah onto the land, the prophet was about at the same point as before, for again God's command came to him. The fact that God repeats his command verbatim is indeed a compelling sermon both of his patience with man and of his rigor. Jonah now knew that he could not escape this God, and so he set out for Nineveh. Here the storyteller has to prepare his listener, who otherwise would not have the proper conception of the inconceivably great size of this city. One needs a full three days to traverse it! And now, there in its midst stood Jonah, preaching, "Yet forty days, and Nineveh shall be overthrown!"

His speech would have been longer; we can think of it as similar to the laments of Isaiah and Ezekiel or to their oracles against the nations. The narrator repeats its content in only a single statement. But one must imagine *how* Jonah preached. We should not be deceived; his sermon is suffused with the same old inflexibility and frostiness that we have observed in him earlier. The sermon's effectiveness, however, was remarkably independent of its preacher's attitude; for the message gripped and frightened the populace. Indeed, as has often happened among the heathen, it caused a mass movement of repentance. The narrator has here given himself opportunity to paint a charming miniature: the matter came before the king, who rose immediately from his throne, laid aside his royal robe, and dressed himself as a penitent. A royal edict was quickly prepared, calling on the people to observe penitential rites. ("By the decree of the king and his nobles: . . .") Everyone was to fast and do penance. Even the herds and the flocks were to take no food or drink, but rather to be veiled in sorrow, everyone crying mightily to God.

Meanwhile Jonah had taken up his abode outside the city, expecting to see shortly a judgment like that which had once fallen on Sodom. But although he was secure enough externally, his cool observation-post was perilous enough from another point of view. For when one thinks about what happened to Lot's wife, one may ask whether God will tolerate such inquisitive contemplation of divine judgment. And in fact Jonah's expectation did not materialize, for God had decided differently about Nineveh: he had seen the city's repentance and forgiven its sin.

And this occasion unleashes Jonah's long restrained agitation! The Hebrew narrator says, "it displeased him greatly," and with his outburst an especially awful terrain comes into view. Now one also learns why Jonah had earlier tried to flee: he had foreseen that God would be gracious and at the decisive moment would leave the prophet in the lurch with his prophetic word unfulfilled. The way Jonah angrily holds up before God the ancient affirmation about God's grace, which the congregation had used in worship for centuries when it presented a thank-offering, sounds almost like the frightful curse of one damned:

> But it displeased Jonah exceedingly, and he was angry. And he prayed to the Lord and said, "I pray thee, Lord, is

Some people fear that God will even save those who have not loved + served him — making them liars because they proclaimed that sinners will burn in hell.

not this what I said when I was yet in my country? That is why I made haste to flee to Tarshish: for I knew that Thou art a gracious God and merciful, slow to anger, and abounding in steadfast love, and repentest of evil." (Jon. 4:1-2)

One sees that he knows all about it. He repeats it like a catechism. But Jonah was deadly serious in his reproach, so serious that he wanted to live no longer. In that he was, to be sure, a man of the old covenant in not throwing his life away himself, but rather in begging God to take it from him. Still, something seems to have given him the will to live, and that was his curiosity about the fate of the city. (The text is visibly uneven here. Verse 5 at least is misplaced, for according to it Jonah is still waiting for God's act. Verse 5, chapter 4, is best read directly after chapter 3:4.) God, however, did not grant Jonah's request. He did not take Jonah's life, but rather treated him as a father might. At the place where the unsatisfied man of God was staying, God now caused a castor oil plant, a large, broad-leafed bush, to grow up quickly. And indeed, as soon as Jonah began to enjoy the shade and coolness of the leafy roof, his bad humor abated, and he became "exceedingly glad because of the plant." But the delight of this man of God soon ceased, for God, the all-knowing and almighty ruler of all creatures, summoned a little worm that attacked the bush, and it quickly withered. To compound this misfortune there now came the scorching east wind so feared in the Near East. As the sun beat upon Jonah's head, he became faint and in a short while so despairing that he once more longed passionately to die. He had accepted the shade from the plant as a small blessing meant for himself; indeed that blessing had completely absorbed his thought. But when that fragile relief was removed from his life, he was enraged, felt himself to be profoundly injured, and was quite incapable of comprehending God's considered, well-meant question about the justification for his wrath: "I do well to be angry, angry enough to die!"

This from the messenger, the executor, so to speak, of

God's thoughts about Nineveh! And now the narrator goes to the limit. He leads us out of twilight, ridiculousness, incomprehensibility, in a word out of everything human, directly to God's heart. God has the final word, and we can do no better than simply repeat that marvelous word here. In its exaltation and grace it fills the entire space; it seems so satisfying and triumphant that any further question about Jonah and his obstinacy becomes superfluous.

> And the Lord said, "You pity the plant, for which you did not labor, nor did you make it grow, which came into being in a night, and perished in a night. And should I not pity Nineveh, that great city, in which there are more than a hundred and twenty thousand persons who do not know their right hand from their left, and also much cattle?" (4:10-11)

II

Before we say anything about the content of this story, we must examine its form. Stories of the prophets, i.e., accounts of noteworthy events that occurred because prophets were there, were long known in Israel; and one can therefore speak about a fixed, literary genre as a traditional narrative form. Our narrative about Jonah is in this sense a story of a prophet. But whereas in the earlier stories of the prophets we have exclusively, or almost so, God's "objective" word or miracle or spiritual work, coming from God, our narrator is concerned with something else: namely, to begin with, the extremely problematic, refractory human nature of the man of God. That in itself is a sign of the relatively late composition of the story. Indeed, our narrative seems to be the latest and strangest flower on that ancient, almost extinct, literary plant. Must one say that here we encounter a clearly accomplished stage in narrative development? That becomes obvious when one observes the care with which the narrator divides the material into two more or less equal parts, chapters one and two on the one hand, and three and four on the other. In the first half we become acquainted with the problem and theme; for the way in which the sea-going people are converted to the living God—because of Jonah, yet completely unrelated to his will—is only a prelude to what happened later at Nineveh because of Jonah. And consider how it is told! With charm and ease and a ghost of a smile such as we scarcely find elsewhere in the Bible! If we were to apply our currect literary conceptions, we would have to say that occasionally—as with the section on Jonah and the castor plant—the story approaches burlesque. But none of that should deceive us. The narrative is about very serious and ultimate matters: about a city whose days are numbered, about God's judgment, about wicked men with hearts of stone, and about God's eternal mercy. True, one cannot read the story without smiling, but because of that the narrator lifts us above all human standards and opinions, almost without our being aware of it. Even Jonah's terrible outburst in chapter 4 is forgiven in God's gracious, fatherly question that follows immediately. With this lightness of touch and strange withdrawal of himself the narrator attempts to portray for us the man Jonah and the whole human landscape as it may have lain before God's eyes.

It has cost the church great effort and much pain to realize that our narrator's purpose is not primarily historical, namely, to recount an actual, historical event. (Even in the 18th century a professor of theology from Helmstadt, who dared to dispute that, was fined one hundred florin and forbidden to hold lectures.) The fact is that one would hopelessly misunderstand the story and even distort it if one were determined to overlook its pedagogic purpose. It is, and is intended to be, a *didactic story*. We have seen that it is attached to the historical person of a prophet, Jonah; and there may be other historical material in it. On the other hand, the motif of the man in the fish seems to be connected with myths of the Mediterranean region. (Heracles, in order to free Hesione, threw himself into the jaws of a sea monster and fought his way out of its body to freedom. The question is discussed fully by H. Schmidt in *Jona*.

Eine Untersuchung zur vergleichenden Religionsgeschichte, 1907.) But we are concerned here not with the history, but with the present form of the story as it lies before us in unusual freshness and brevity.

If we understand the narrative of the prophet Jonah as a didactic story, it exhibits manifestly both negatively and positively something typical, something of general validity. That is quite obvious. The scenes of Jonah in the ship and Jonah before Nineveh are quite similar. Both times we see the heathen paying close attention, honestly struggling and praying in their need, while Jonah stays at a distance. One time he sleeps; the other time (when one wishes he had slept!) he sits before the city and follows what happens with a wicked interest. And in this wicked aloofness there appears the castor plant that makes Jonah glad. Its bit of shade and coolness absorb him completely, and he becomes discomfited when the plant withers. (Men of God at all times had their castor plants about which they had to be anxious!) But what does it all mean? Where is the narrative tending?

Now in Near Eastern didactic stories one must guard oneself against formulating "the" teaching too onesidedly, as though stuck on the point of a needle (parables of Jesus!). As a rule there are several levels to the lesson. But, to speak quite generally, a warm sympathy for the heathen is of course the decisive characteristic of the whole narrative. It is remarkable that *they* are the ones who seize the initiative aboard the ship, *they* press Jonah with the question about God and suspect instinctively that their peril is on his account. And the repentance of the Ninevites is told with equal affection. Observe how the psychological aspects of their humanity are described: for them, the seafarers and the Ninevites alike, everything is simple and transparent. But Jonah is problematic and psychologically exceedingly complex. He becomes most sinister when he expresses the matters of his faith in the ancient confessional formulations with which his behavior stands in such sharp contrast. (What a psychological and religious monster is that interweaving of prayer and anger and confession in the words of chapter 4!)

Of course there is caricature in all of it, and one has consequently spoken of the satiric character of the booklet. But that judgment presupposes an admixture of sharpness and bitterness that is completely absent from the booklet. What remains, then, is only the question about the "seriousness" of the teaching in all of that. For this one must begin, of course, with the conclusion of the booklet, for clearly the narrator here formulates the essential "teaching" of the whole story. If we say, however, that the teaching has to do with "the universalism of God's saving purpose," as is often said, there is in this a dangerous rock for us modern readers. Often enough one has presented the matter as though the narrator wished to point to a general religious truth in contrast to any dogmatic folly. But one cannot warn too earnestly against understanding the narrative as product of a cheap enlightenment. ("That narrow-minded Israel! How could it believe that God was concerned with it in a different sense than he is with the other peoples of the world?")

The book of Jonah stands at the end of Israel's history of faith. It speaks to those who know what community and election are, not to those who know on their own that God's saving purpose is "of course universal." It does not point, therefore, to a general "religious truth" which a person can and should accept. Our narrator does not touch upon Israel's covenant and election, but he does point out one of the most difficult temptations the community faces. There is such a thing—strange psychology of God's people!—as a malevolence of faith and a bitterness toward the heathen. This is not a thoughtless malevolence, which would lie somewhat outside faith, but rather malevolence of faith itself and the way it acts. It is quite clear that Jonah had well-understood God's ways with his people, and that understanding became the basis and motivation for his disobedience. The book does not present a character development, as we generally understand it in modern literature, but it shows something else: the gradual dawning of an appraisal. This man's nature and way of

more concerned with personal blessings than with blessings shown to others

thinking are more and more crassly revealed. This Jonah (namely, Israel), who begrudges the heathen God's goodness, is so filled with joy and anger over the castor plant that he is unable to share in God's thoughts and feelings about Nineveh. These divine thoughts and feelings are undoubtedly, in the final analysis, of supreme importance for our narrator. They cannot be thwarted by any circumstances, and even the absurd acts of a Jonah cannot hinder God's work. (In my judgment this thought is thematically pre-eminent, not the "problem" whether God will graciously rescind his judgment, expressed by the prophet, against a sinful city when the city repents. H. Schmidt, "Absicht und Entstehungszeit des Buches Jona," *Theol. Studien und Kritiken,* 1906, p. 192.) And because God's saving purpose is triumphant, all the idiosyncrasies of his witness on earth can be told without gloom and with a smile.

III

We must now address ourselves to what is perhaps the most difficult aspect of this book for our understanding, namely to the so-called psalm of Jonah (2:3-10). Old Testament scholars are agreed that it is a later addition, which was naturally inserted after the words, "Jonah prayed from the belly of the fish." It troubles us that the situation of this prayer does not agree with that of Jonah. The prayer was obviously spoken after Jonah's deliverance and was uttered, according to verse 9, in the temple at Jerusalem. But perhaps most troublesome is its psychological incredibility, for these pious and thankful words do not accord with Jonah's obstinacy, which was worse afterward than before. Still, one must ask whether the prayer is really nothing more than a more or less unfortunate and incongruous addition, inserted because it contains language about the heart of the seas, waves, and seaweed.

Whoever inserted the prayer apparently believed that Jonah could have prayed in that way, and in fact ancient

Israel seems to have thought about the relationship between prayer and life differently than we do. Does not every attentive reader of the Psalms ask about their biographical backgrounds? Still, in spite of their most personal style in the first person, one can scarcely recognize behind all those confessions the actual vicissitudes or sufferings their authors experienced. Those suppliants made much more use of traditional images and forms of speech than we are often willing to believe; they took from their services of worship forms and formulas that had become conventions after centuries of use, and they found for themselves a place in them where they could present their own personal needs. Those descriptions of being cast into the depths of the sea, of abiding in the world of death, or, on the other hand, of complete religious uprightness—are they to be understood as being biographically veracious, in the sense that they report actually-experienced suffering or really-accomplished obedience? Now that would be difficult to prove. What is clear, however, is that the personal reappears somewhat brokenly in the form of objective images and formulas. It is also clear that many of these statements transcend what was actually experienced. The suppliants often describe themselves as the ideal or original righteous sufferers. They thus somewhat withdraw from themselves in prayer, in spite of all personal urgency; and they hold up an image of the ideal righteous or suffering person, which we should not assume corresponds with their own personal circumstances.

That is the case with Jonah, and we have to let the question about the agreement between Jonah's psychological or biographical state and his prayer be answered as it may. The Jonah here at prayer is indeed a different Jonah. He is the Jonah who is and has been declared righteous before God; he is the Jonah who presents himself not only as he really is in God's sight, but rather as God in his forgiving grace actually sees him: as redeemed and thankful. The psalm of Jonah thus touches upon a great mystery by pointing to that other Jonah, Israel, who is much more important before God than the dubious Jonah of the story. These two Jonah figures, however, do not simply separate into two. It is quite possible that the righteous one enters into the disobedient one and lends him his voice. And when such thanksgiving, strange though it be, comes from lips that are otherwise impious—even when that praise is seriously contradicted by the life of the person in question who does not, perhaps, really understand at all what he is saying—there the sun of divine comfort does shine, even though behind clouds. (Some characteristics of the book of Jonah are mentioned in the New Testament, especially in Matthew 12:40 f. and Luke 11:30. That does not, however, give us the only correct interpretative key to the matter. Our interpretation alone should have shown that Delitzsch's fine statement is justified: "The book of Jonah is a historial painting of profound psychological, dogmatic and typical significance, through the dusky background of which shines Christ Jesus, the Savior not only of Jews but of all peoples." *Op. cit.*, p. 122.)

8

THE STORY
OF JOB'S SUFFERING

*(Evangelical address over Southwest German radio,
October 1961.)*

The book of Job is an ancient poetical work of huge size.
An ancient poetical work! Need I say that we may not
approach it with the same definite expectations we would
bring to a modern work of literature? We should not have
any definite expectation, but rather leave ourselves open
as well as we can to its uniqueness, its particular literary
art, and its religious problems. The work consists, as
everyone can see, of two very different parts: the more
popular narrative framework, and the dialogues. The
first is epic prose, while the dialogues move along in the
most exalted poetic style.

Today we are concerned only with the epic prose story
(Job 1–2; 42:7-17). According to it, Job was an
immensely wealthy sheikh, as we would call him today,
who lived on the eastern edge of Palestine. But not only
was he rich, he was also a good and devout man who
with his large family led a life deeply rooted in
religious, patriarchal customs. Thus the reader hears at
once what he always learns with satisfaction: the
harmony of good conduct and well-being. But the reader
also knows that a great problem will arise precisely on
this point. The first segment of the narrative has
mentioned only conditions, i.e., the facts about Job. One
can therefore, without further ado, characterize these
first five verses as the exposition. The actual story then

begins, and its first scene takes us up to heaven. (We are instinctively reminded of the scenes in a stage play.)

In heaven no sweet atmosphere prevails. It is the day of audience, when the angels of heaven must appear before the king of heaven to report and receive orders. Among them appears the adversary. Here we must pay strict attention and guard against confusing the figure presented by the poet with popular conceptions about the devil. The adversary is one of the heavenly beings, indeed God takes a special interest in him. God questions him before the adversary can make his report. To the question, whence has he come, the adversary answers, somewhat pertly one must say, "from going to and fro on the earth." Even so, we infer from that answer that his task was to traverse the earth with his eyes open for anything wrong that might be going on anywhere in the broad realm of the heavenly king. He had to report whatever he saw. But God, the lord, was not deterred by the adversary's somewhat noncommital and evidently evasive answer. God asked directly about Job, the completely just and blameless godly man, in whom even the adversary's sharp eye could find nothing bad. That was, of course, a blunt challenge for the adversary, who now abandons at once his reserve: "Does Job fear God for nought?" This question falls on the scene like a stone. The adversary does not contest Job's piety at all. He raises an extremely interesting point, for he poses the question of motives. When things go well, when God blesses one in everything, it is easy to be devout.

Behind this argument stands, of course, the question of whether there is a "special reward" for piety. Is man not an egoist in everything, including his piety? We ask incidentally: Was the adversary's counter-question unjust, even diabolical? No, it was a genuine, sober question, and with this objection the adversary maintained God's interest. God immediately gives him a free hand to investigate the matter. God, therefore, is interested in having the question clarified; for he has vouched for Job and the genuineness of his piety in the hearing of all heavenly beings. The adversary makes his departure.

The next scene takes place on earth. This technique on the part of the narrator of working with two stages, so to speak, one heavenly and one earthly, gives the reader background for the entire happening. He now knows the background in heaven for Job's testing, while Job, of course, has no inkling of all that. The strokes of misfortune fall upon him dreadfully; scarcely has one messenger made his report of disaster before the next one appears: the oxen, the sheep, the camels, and finally Job's children fall victim before the feared cyclone. "Then Job arose, and rent his robe . . . and fell upon the ground, and worshiped. 'Naked I came from my mother's womb, and naked shall I return; the Lord gave, and the Lord has taken away; blessed be the name of the Lord.' "

It would surely be quite wrong to consider Job an impassive stoic, an acrobat, so to speak, in self-control, one able to keep his composure in an almost superhuman manner. No, Job is quite human; horror overcomes him; he is profoundly injured and makes that clearly visible in the customary ceremonies of sorrow. But in and despite his great suffering that bows him low, he remains secure in his piety. His statement, the Lord gives, the Lord has taken away, is not particularly profound; but it is quite simple and true, and its logic is plainly cogent. If God has given, he can also take away. To that Job submits.

If we think back to the previous scene in heaven, it is clear that all the heavenly beings who heard God's conversation with the adversary are watching Job in suspense and waiting for his reaction. Job held fast to God; in no way did he jilt God or his faith, as the adversary had expected he would. We await, therefore, in suspense the development of God's second conversation with the adversary; for what else can the adversary do, the reader thinks, than admit defeat? But surprisingly he is not at all defeated. When God reminds him, with the clear overtone of reproach, that Job held fast to his piety afterward as well as beforehand, the adversary answers: "Skin for skin! All that a man has he will give for his life." Again, that is in its way a powerful statement. Man, as the adversary thinks he knows him, is a cold egoist. In the last analysis he values his life above everything else, and for its sake he will jettison everything. The first trial and its result, therefore, signify nothing. If a man's life is threatened, however, then he is capable of anything, and then his essential cynicism will come to light.

A terrible assertion! But things proceed as in the first scene: God recognizes the force of the argument. The adversary should arrange further testing. Thereafter Job is stricken with terrible sores. He has to leave the company of the healthy. In silence he accepts the lot of the ritually unclean and places himself on the rubbish heap outside the settlement, where he receives a visit from his wife. When she sees Job suffering in such great misery, she advises him tersely: "Curse God, and die!" Now that is scarcely to be understood as an abyss of human insensibility. The woman is only human. So long as she believes she can expect to have something from God, she holds with him, but only that long. Thus it comes to pass exactly as the adversary had predicted it would—for the representative of the average man, but not for Job! He flares up at this suggestion: "You speak as one of the foolish women would speak. Shall we receive good at the hand of God, and shall we not receive evil?" What we said earlier is again true now: this should not be seen as the supreme result of self-control, but simply as a quite simple and self-evident statement. Job is so secure in his relationship to God that he really does not understand his wife's suggestion at all. One cannot simply affirm God as the giver of good and then hesitate to accept suffering at his hand. With that the adversary is defeated. God has no further conversations with him, for the matter is clear enough. In the ancient prose work the restoration of Job's prosperity and health, which we now read in the 42nd chapter of the book, must have been related quickly. "And Job died, an old man, and full of days."

The prose narrative about Job bears all the marks of a didactic story. It is concerned first of all simply with the question of whether there is such a thing as genuine, perfect, and selfless piety. And when God, the Lord, answers this question affirmatively in advance for the adversary, the story goes on to show how a person vindicated the word of honor with which God had vouched for him, as Herder once beautifully expressed it. The adversary is essentially a minor figure in the whole story. He is not God's diabolical antagonist, but rather a kind of heavenly, public prosecutor with whom God discourses and whose arguments he takes seriously. He has no other authority. Significantly, Job does not say, "The Lord has given, Satan has taken away." Job is dealing exclusively with God. But what Job says is decisive, for—again Herder has formulated it splendidly—this Job suffers as God's pride and joy. This man, cast upon the rubbish heap, who, as we have said, had no inkling of the antecedents in heaven that led to his suffering or of the consequences that indeed depended on his words—this man is the best witness for God, just because he took a stand for God's sake and gave God his due.

Into the old prose narrative have been worked wide-ranging dialogues between Job and his friends. These additions, in the universal opinion of scholars, were made later. Since they have their own importance and their own theological topics, we will treat them specially in a later broadcast.

9

THE DISCUSSION
ABOUT JOB'S SUFFERING

*(Evangelical address over Southwest German radio,
October 1961.)*

As any reader may see and as we mentioned recently,
the book of Job is divided into two relatively unequal
parts: the prose narrative about Job who is completely
secure in and devoted to God; and the great section of
dialogues (39 chapters), which were evidently inserted
later into the simple prose narrative and which open up a
whole new horizon of religious problems and temptations
respecting the ancient, didactic narrative.

So far as the form is concerned, the later work has been
incorporated into the earlier almost without a seam.
There we were told that three friends visited the
sore-covered Job at the rubbish heap outside the
settlement, where he had betaken himself as one
unclean. And then the narrator added: "And when they
saw him from afar, they did not recognize him; and they
raised their voices and wept; . . . And they sat with him
on the ground seven days and seven nights, and no one
spoke a word to him, for they saw that his suffering was
very great" (2:12-13). Is that not a monumental gesture of
sympathy, this silence on the part of the men who had
come to comfort Job? They analyze nothing; they first of
all simply recognize the full extent of his suffering. That
silence will not be everything, but when they speak later
they will do so as those who previously had long been
silent. The first one to break the long and terrible silence

is Job, and now with chapter 3 we have crossed into the younger work. We meet a different Job. He curses his life and the day he was born: "Why was I not stillborn. Why is light given to him that is in misery, who longs for death, but it comes not?" This complaint of Job's is to some extent the overture to the great, three part dialogue that now follows.

Every one of the friends speaks, and the poet lets Job answer each one. Thus Job speaks much more frequently than any one of them does; and that is as the poet intended, for the dominant import of the dialogues lies in the great monologues of Job. In them the poet expresses his most important thoughts, but that should not mislead us into underrating the significance of the friends' speeches. A rather primitive interpretation, one that is unfortunately widespread, makes everything the friends say false or even imputes to them hypocrisy wherever possible. Things are not quite that simple.

The first speech of Eliphaz is a masterpiece of careful, pastoral address. He speaks to Job just as Job has instructed and comforted others when it was necessary. And then he advises him: "I would seek God, and to God would I commit my cause" (5:8). "Behold, happy is the man whom God reproves; therefore despise not the chastening of the Almighty. For he wounds, but he binds up; he smites, but his hands heal" (5:17-18). Should one say things like that to Job? Eliphaz does not have a general prescription, but he echoes the experience of the community and believes Job would do well to consider it. Later in the 8th chapter Bildad admonishes Job in the same vein to consider seriously the wisdom and experience of previous generations: "For we are but of yesterday, and know nothing." Whoever speaks about suffering, Bildad thinks, cannot do so as though he were the first one ever to suffer! And was that not the weakness of Job's position? He fights his fight with God in icy isolation, as though God had never revealed his will and his purposes for mankind to the patriarchs or Moses or the prophets. Job is living the life of a man beset with temptations, without a history and without a community, a man cast completely on his own resources, to whom the entire, rich tradition of the faith of his forebears had nothing more to say. That is also the basic reason for his inability to listen to his friends. The reader has the depressing feeling that these men, who seem to be speaking together, are in fact carrying on monologues, as though there were a wall between them. They are like men who cannot escape the prison of their own thoughts and experiences. In what follows I must limit myself to suggesting two lines of argument in these monologues from the book of Job, in which one can observe, however difficult it may be for the reader, some progression in thought. What is remarkable, though, is that these two lines intersect in such a way that they cannot again be brought into agreement.

Immediately after Eliphaz's first speech, Job answers with an idea which he can thereafter almost not surrender: "The arrows of the Almighty are in me." He feels himself transfixed by God's arrows, "My spirit drinks their poison; the terrors of God are arrayed against me" (6:4). This God, of whom Job is thinking, is man's enemy; he threatens and terrifies him. This God is a dark God before whom man is always worsted. How could a man ever be right before him, "If one wished to contend with him, one could not answer him once in a thousand times" (9:3). "Behold, he snatches away; who can hinder him? Who will say to him 'what doest thou?' " (9:12). But if, on the one hand, intense fear of God's obscurity grips him, still, and this is the other line of thought, Job cannot be free of him. Indeed he is nothing short of being fascinated with God's greatness that surpasses all human comprehension.

But Job scarcely gets excited for this God before his friends, since he feels rejected by him, indeed profoundly threatened. He cannot explain to himself this interest that God has in man: "What is man, that thou dost make so much of him? How long wilt thou not look away from me, nor let me alone till I swallow my spittle?" (7:17, 19) This negative line, i.e., the line of a growing terror before God, reaches a certain nadir in chapter 16, where God's presence over him is distorted into a devilish face: God gnashes his teeth, sharpens his eyes against him (the Greek translation speaks here of eye-daggers), "he seized me by the neck . . . he slashes open my kidneys . . . he pours out my gall on the ground . . . my face is red with weeping, and on my eyelids is deep darkness" (vv. 9-16). Job has here stumbled onto the dark side of God, the terrors of which only a few, perhaps, experience in the course of millennia.

But now, in a way that is scarcely imaginable any longer, he leaps over to the other line of thought. With incomprehensible boldness he becomes convinced that God will not permit his creature to fall. "Even now, behold, my witness is in heaven, . . . my eye pours out tears to God, that he would maintain the right of a man with God" (vv. 19-21), and a little later, "I know that my Redeemer lives" (19:25). That is one of the highpoints of the other line of thought. Here Job has found the God who esteems him and does not destroy him like a worm.

But the matter is not so simply edifying as that. Job stands in a most dramatic crisis of faith; his image of God has almost taken on two aspects, for he invokes God the friend against God the enemy who is destroying him. At the end of the 31st chapter this certainty has risen to a dizzying religious self-assurance: "Oh, that I had one to hear me! (Here is my signature! let the Almighty answer me!) . . . like a prince I would approach him." Here one can see quite clearly what for Job was ultimately at stake. Not, as is so often said, a solution to the problem of suffering, but rather his relationship to God. The question is simply whether this God who has become so incomprehensible and terrible to him is his God in whom he can trust.

God answers Job's final challenge with a speech that showers him with a cascade of questions. What do you understand about creation, the light, the rain, the stars, and especially the animals? Can you provide for them? Can you supervise when the mountain goats shall bear young and what the activity of the wild ass shall be? The reader cannot mistake the fine overtone, that man's reason will not help him and considerations of utility come to nought. God pours out over the steppe the rain, the most costly items in the household of nature, and the wild asses that live far from the human scene cannot really be fitted into any human system of value. But above all, the change in the situation is remarkable. The questioner suddenly finds himself the questioned and pressed at once into a fully defensive position. No doubt, this flood of questions contains at first something very simple, namely, a sovereign dismissal of Job. But one would be obtuse not to apprehend something else from the sitation, namely, an overtone of God's joy in his creation to which his fatherly care binds him. This flood of questions which drives Job into a corner is not, however, oppressive. Indeed, does not God woo Job in order to let him participate in his joy as creator? Let the world be filled with riddles; these riddles repose in God's heart! Is not *that* the teaching of God's long address: man can never comprehend God's world rule, but he can treat it with reverence. And Job answers in that spirit: "I know that thou canst do all things. . . . I had heard of thee by the hearing of the ear, but now my eye sees thee; therefore I despise myself, and repent in dust and ashes" (42:2, 5-6). He had heard of God by hearsay only, and now God has found him. God's address, not some greedy glimpse of divine mystery, has given Job value. There is more. He receives value from looking into God's heart where all the mysteries of the world and human life reside.

10

THE MYSTERY
OF OLD TESTAMENT ISRAEL

(Undated lecture manuscript. This version probably dates from the sixties.)

To formulate the theme this way may suggest a thriller. But the title can be understood in a scientific sense as well, not as a sensational attempt to solve a mystery, but as the much more modest effort to see that mystery properly, to assess it, paraphrase it, and define it more precisely within a broader context.

For there is a mystery. Every people, of course, harbors a mystery, something ultimate and inexplicable that is more than the sum of their natural and historical preconditions. But the mystery of Old Testament Israel is on quite a different level. Israel engaged and upset the peoples that came into contact with her. Among the host of reproaches, absurd in part and malevolent in part, that have been leveled against the Jews throughout the long history of anti-Semitism, that of amixia, "unsociableness," "separateness," which played a great role in the Hellenistic Syrian world, is perhaps the most factual and serious. In that reproach is expressed the amazement and then also the indignation of those who suddenly encountered a national community that was unwilling to enter unreservedly into the varied economic, intellectual, and finally religious exchanges that had become matter of course in the motley political world of Hellenism. The basis for this indeed striking reticence lies, of course, in the religious conceptions of Judaism at that time. The heathen, Hellenistic world was most tolerant of the religious cults to which its various groups of people subscribed; and it was not its way at all to bar access to new cults. It expected of new religious communities only one thing, namely, the same tolerance and, at the least, relative recognition of the cults already there. Precisely this was not possible for the Jews who were spreading ever wider throughout the ancient world, even if they had to pay a price for their own existence. That brings us directly to this mystery of Israel which so enigmatically has made this people a stranger among the nations and their religions.

What is its basis?

Ancient Israel was a people like others. Doubtless it possessed an unusual gift, but still one must hesitate to see therein Israel's distinctive character. Like other peoples, Israel passed through stages of growth: a period of archaic freshness (the times of Moses and the Judges), then a period of becoming intellectually self-aware, a kind of enlightenment and humanism, and finally a period of regression in her creative powers, a period of restoration, compilation, and integration. Those phenomena are well known to the historian. But there is still enough that is without analogy and quite singular to startle the student of religion.

Let me now approach a point at which I believe something of the mystery of Israel becomes particularly clear and which later remains the exciting, specific point that distinguishes Israel in the world of religions: the absence of images in her worship of God. One usually grossly misconstrues this command, as though it were directed against externals and toward a spiritual, inner worship of God. But this separation of the spiritual and material proceeds from Greek intellectual presuppositions that were unknown to Israel. As a rule, throughout the various religious cults, men knew precisely that the deity could not simply be identified with a wooden or gold-covered figure. But even a very spiritual conception of the deities did not prevent those worshipers from erecting images; idols are not a sign of religious infantilism at all. More properly one would have to characterize the idol as a mediator of the spirituality of the God in question. No, in this commandment against making images the concern is not to separate invisible from visible; i.e., the command does not represent a stage in human knowledge which every people and every religion reaches, nor does it teach a general, religious truth. The worship of images is placed together, in fact, with murder, adultery, and idolatry.

We have to begin elsewhere, not with the question, to what extent the cultic idea of God is adequate and adequately expressed, but rather with the question, what does it declare. Between the image and the worshiper something happens, something proceeds, something comes to a person. All images are mediums for the spirit, and images of the gods are even more so. Israel did not contest that. Religiously speaking, the deity reveals itself in the image. Permit me for once to remove all distinctions in the history of religions and express the matter this way: according to the belief of all religions that worship the deity in images, man lives in a world full of miracles and terrors. He would be lost without the gods and thanks them because they reveal themselves everywhere; everywhere they open up their mysteries and allow man to receive their blessing. The world would be a frightfully dark room; but windows from the world of the gods have been opened, and man lives by their light. Every place in the world can become transparent, so to speak, become a symbol, i.e., an authorized or empowered declaration of God. The deity can reveal itself in trees, animals, and stars. The image is the medium between God and man; it is the bearer of revelation. One can build altars to the deity, for the god's mysteries are infinite. We encounter this faith most highly spiritualized in Goethe.

To all of that Israel said no! No Jew will deny that the world discloses abysmal mysteries. But he will deny that they are the revelation of God, the living God. Here, in all these cults with their profound symbolism, the concern is always nothing more than a conversation of the creature with itself. God is much more concealed from man and much nearer to him!

Think of something as simple and yet as remarkable as the ancient command about the sabbath. The fact is that thousands of things occupy a person in life; claims are made upon him from every side, and commitments bind him. In every one of these obligations, especially in a man's work wherever it is taken seriously, there abides an almost demonic power. It wills to be the only lord of a person's life and thus, with frightful ease, becomes an idol. Human work, of course, never ends; it knows no conclusion, requires continual perfecting, and so it levies an exclusive claim of lordship on a person; and precisely this is what God crosses out. Neither the dignity nor the seriousness of work is touched, only this exclusive claim to lordship. Week after week a man is to set aside one day and thereby raise a signal that all of his work, all of his earthly obligations, however honorable they may be, are not ultimate concerns by which he is imprisoned, that above them all stands the living God with his majestic claim on the man. Is not this command about the sabbath simply a way to be serious about the command, "You shall have no other gods before me"? Thus the Old Testament shows us God, whom we do not know otherwise, as the God who makes a claim above all claims upon a man and his whole life. Perhaps we feel coerced, something in us resists this distraint. The devout men of the old covenant, however, were convinced that man belongs to God and must serve and obey him.

All of this, this knowledge about the profound folly of all image-worship, this resolute refusal to recognize the various and enticing voices from the depths of creation as a revelation from God, this, that Israel yielded to no sacred symbolism, no mythologizing, and no deification of the world, is the loneliness of Israel in the world of religions. With that we touch directly on the mystery of

Israel. In all of that we are concerned not with religious or philosophical premises, but rather with something second, to some extent a consequence, a result. Something had happened before all that. Israel found herself drawn by God from the start into a history. Indeed she found herself commandeered by God so inescapably that all attempts to elude this grip, of which there were more than a few, remained unsuccessful. This history—and now we go a step further—was, of course, no dumb, anonymous, fated course of events. Rather, God personally drew near to this history of his with Israel in his word that he addressed to Israel, and he chose her to be his partner in conversation. One could wonder whether this certainty of being drawn by God into conversation should not be considered an expression of dizzying religious arrogance. But, on the other hand, one must reflect that this witness by Israel to the divine word that she experienced is in great part a witness against herself, a witness to her fear and despair at this word and this address. But in the long centuries of this conversation with God, Israel developed a profound and, in the history of religions, a particular knowledge. She learned that nothing is so necessary to human life as to hear this divine word. "To Thee, O Lord, I call; my rock, be not deaf to me, lest, if thou be silent to me, I become like those who go down to the Pit" (Ps. 28:1). Here it is expressed: when God is silent, man is undone and falls prey to death. The times when God's word was "rare" in the land (I Sam. 3:1) were times of confusion and depression. The book of Deuteronomy, in the style of a long valedictory by Moses, mounts to the elementary statement: The word which I command you today "is no trifle for you, but it is your life" (Deut. 32:47). Life! Pause for a moment. How uniform in religions is the conception of an inner-worldly power, a mystery that is holy in itself and could become accessible to man through some rite, myth, or speculation! And how cool and clear the voice of the Old Testament: "Man does not live by bread alone, but by everything that proceeds out of the mouth of the Lord" (Deut. 8:3). Man lives, therefore, from the fact that God speaks to him. Where God is silent, hunger for God's word arises, and a terrible weakness comes over man (Amos 8:11 f.).

That delineates somewhat more clearly, perhaps, what we have called the mystery of Israel. We see in Israel of the Old Testament a people that is increasingly occupied with the word of God. Not, to be sure, always to its own honor; sometimes refusing it, but even so, occupied and engaged in this conversation with God, not released from it! Think now of the book of Psalms as the incomparable document of this conversation between a people and God, about everything there is to discuss, the world, nations, the past, the future, suffering, sin, and death. Israel carried on this conversation in every situation: at times of performing an obligation, of thanksgiving, of self-forgetting worship, and in the darkest nights of despair. There are psalms so poor that they do not bring strength and assurance to the petition, but display only distress. Rilke once declared in a most beautiful way that the Psalter is one of the very "few books in which one engrosses oneself completely, however distraught and disordered and disturbed one may be" (Letters to His Publisher, p. 247).

But the Psalms are by no means the only document of Israel's continuing conversation with God. The entire Old Testament can easily be understood as the literary expression of this conversation. Let me make that somewhat clearer. What Israel understood by word of God was precisely the opposite of a philosophical truth; it was always a historical event. "The Word of the Lord came." This word did not mediate knowledge of higher worlds and was not at all concerned with the transcendent, but rather with eminently immanent, historically immanent matters. It contains instructions, consolation, and above all disclosures of divine plans for history. "He made known his ways to Moses, his acts to the people of Israel" (Ps. 103:7). The word of Amos is even more emphatic. "Surely the Lord God does nothing, without revealing his secret to his servants the prophets" (3:7). Think what that means: Israel makes the claim to understand her history, to understand it in God's sight. That is, she sees herself, after looking back on quite definite events, in the situation of speaking about quite definite divine plans, foundations or condemnations, in a word, about the direct activity of God.

In that connection Israel has a term for history which does not correspond at all with our profane science of history. History for Israel is not simply the sum of all existing memories of what has been (*Historie*). On the one hand Israel seems to have had a profound understanding of the riddle, the inexplicability of what we call history, indeed world history; for she seems to have reckoned this dimension, if anywhere, to the unformed movements of primeval chaos. History, in a qualified sense, was for Israel always and only that part of the way on which God had accompanied her, whether he was supporting, saving, or judging her. To speak about her history and to try to present it anew at every stage in her realization of faith was meaningful for Israel only when her history was set in relief by God himself.

Indeed, in Israel's restless reflection about her history, and in her effort to understand herself in history before God, she became aware at a certain stage of a great mystery: the actual motor of her history, the power that actually formed this history and drove it forward (we will say something particular about that below) was God's word. We heard it above. It is not an empty word, it is creative. This word that invades history over and over again, especially the prophetic word, gave Israel's history its movement and its goal. In fact, Israel did not present her history, as that usually happens in more or less heroic style, but rather as the history of a people from whose hand had been taken the freedom to give shape to its own history, whose history God had invaded with his declaration, "My thoughts are not your thoughts, neither are your ways my ways" (Isa. 55:8). At the beginning of this history was no great human act, no heroic act for freedom. Rather, at the beginning was God, and at the end would be God.

When I spoke just now about God and his word that formed history and set it in relief, I did not mean to say that everything in Israel's history was therefore clear to her. In a certain respect, indeed, the opposite could better be maintained. Does not Israel's literary bequest show us in ever newer form that Israel, precisely because of her encounter with God, was led into a region of religious riddles and quite specific temptations, and of course quite specific joys as well, all of which were unknown to other peoples and religions? The questions and realizations that opened up in this conversation between Israel and God have no analogy in the history of religions. They have their roots exclusively in the self-revelation of a God who confronted Israel's faith with more and more profound riddles.

And with that we come closer to what theologians call the hiddenness of God. They do not mean by that simply the abundantly familiar fact that God is amply hidden from natural man, the truism of human blindness with respect to God, but rather something much more exciting; namely, the fact that God, precisely where he reveals himself, where he personally encounters a man, conceals himself from the man in that very act. In his self-revelation God judges and destroys all our ideas about God, all the principal images and criteria of value that we accept about him. We can, on our own, imagine only idols, of course. Thus for Christian faith the cross of Christ is the place of God's most profound concealment, i.e., his impotence and shame, and at the same time the place of the revelation of his most exalted majesty. If there is any truth in that, then every revelation of the living God carries with it the temptation that follows as a shadow follows light. The knowledge of God's hiddenness does not, therefore, stand at the end of all thought like a great wall, but rather at the beginning of all knowledge of God.

In this matter we have to think in the Old Testament first of all about the so-called patriarchal stories, which are anything but edifying tales for children, because they make considerable claims on theological understanding.

Abraham set out from home under the burden of an enormous, programmatic word of God; the first thing he met in the Promised Land was famine (Gen. 12). The assuring, divine words of promise are repeated, but their fulfillment seems to recede in a puzzling way before what is striding across the future; and when the heir to this whole promise is finally born, God orders Abraham himself to sacrifice him on Mt. Moriah. In the story of Isaac's sacrifice the knowledge of an extreme and almost unbearable dark side of God had solidified; it is the knowledge of possibilities in which God seems to arise as the enemy and destroyer of his own work. When that solidification begins, and in the continuation of the story it will not be missing, then Israel is to know that God is testing her faith. That is what Genesis 22 has to say to those who read it.

But this was only a first word, an initial step on a road into even more terrible "darkness of God." There follows that word of Isaiah about the strange, unusual work of God. There is the passion of Jeremiah, descending step by step into an icy abandonment by God; and the struggle of Job, in which Israel's conversation with God leaves all conventions behind and enters at times into a blasphemous, derisory, and slanderous outburst ("How long wilt thou not look away from me, nor let me alone till I swallow my spittle?" 7:19). And the Christian will add, there are Gethsemane and Golgotha.

Still everything would be totally distorted if we were to see this night of God and this increase in temptations as the sum total of ancient Israel's history of faith. In fact talk about Israel's breakdown has already entered the theological jargon. And how false an oversimplification it is! God never let Israel fall, and Israel never asserted that he did. God remained the God of Israel in spite of everything; and Israel never stopped addressing God as Thou, even in her darkest hours. Indeed she even said that God gives songs in the night (Job 35:10). The songs of Israel! Where else do we find this devotion, this disregard of one's own interest, this self-abandon in song, in singing simply about God's glory and that of his creation?

That is again something peculiar to the Old Testament. Israel, in conversation with her God, learned to see and understand the world. Not only was God revealed to her; the world about her was also revealed. The myths fell away and the madness of images, and the world was seen as creation, the opposite of God. Man too was revealed in the light of God, much more clearly and convincingly than he could know himself in all his philosophical efforts at self-knowledge. Or is one to say that the story of the Fall, with its penetrating psychological clarity, with its discerning questions (What is shame, and what is the fear of man? What do the disturbances in the life of the woman and the man mean?) is not a radical disclosure of human nature? Here, in the light of the revealed God of Israel, in strict relationship to belief in creation, arose that unbelievable realistic picture of man—which the whole western world has made its own and about which we moderns gladly forget—that man is not free or at will to see himself that way. This image of man is based on definite, theological presuppositions; and where they vanish, there appears in its place almost of necessity a caricature, a kind of modern mythological man. But all these kings, swordsmen, princes, priests, and bankrupts—and not to be forgotten, these glorious women from all classes of society—bustle about on this most human of all stages. This cheerful poise, as one would often like to call it, in the portrayal of everything human, be it exalted or abased, glorious or frightful; this poise even in the portrayal of great guilt and crime, as in the story of Joseph, is neither spiritual impartiality nor moral indifference. No, to see man in this way means to know that God has seen him first; and wherever God has spoken, human sentiments and resentments have become uninteresting. There alone can that incomparable freedom and breadth in the representation of man unfold. That seems paradoxical, to be sure. Only in this light, before this hidden and yet revealed confrontation, does man take his actual measure. Only here does he achieve size and interest; only here do all the immanent possibilities of his self-perception burst out of the riddle of his existence.

Nietzsche recognized that in a marvelous way.

In the Jewish "Old Testament," the book of divine justice, there are men, matters and utterances in a style so grand that Greek and Indian literatures have nothing to compare with it. One is terrified and reverent in the presence of these enormous vestiges of what man once was; and one will have one's sad thoughts, thereby, about ancient Asia and its small, semi-dependent half-island, Europe, which would like to stand for human "progress" as compared with Asia. Of course, anyone who is himself a delicate, tame pet that knows only the needs of a pet (like our modern well-bred men, including the Christians of "well-bred" Christianity) such a one will neither be astonished nor distressed at that ruin. A taste for the Old Testament is a stone of testing with respect to "great" and "small." (*Beyond Good and Evil*, No. 52)

But there is one thing Nietzsche did not mention. This warrant for speaking quite so grandiosely about man was seen by Israel as proceeding from a definite form of faith. Indeed, that is the single possibility that gives us confidence. Here is man, seeking to comprehend himself and his world, determining his place, his existence in the world, his way of thinking. And now there is the open question, whether he thereby stumbles onto the transcendent, i.e., whether this definition of his existence brings him into contact with the divine world. Some consider it possible and necessary, while the more materialistically-oriented dispute it. Man's understanding of the Old and New Testaments goes in precisely the opposite direction. It does not proceed from man and ask from that starting point about contact with God; it begins with God and says that man can only be understood at all if one begins with God, and every other form of understanding man can lead only to distortions or diminutions. Man has his origin in God's heart, as the creation story declares, when it has God say, "let us make man. . . ." At the creation God took the model for man from the upper, divine world, something he did not do for his other creative works. Man is thus a creature who can be understood only from above and who, having severed his relationship with God, can regain and maintain his humanity only by hearkening to the divine word. Thus there emerges in the confessions of the Psalms, and especially too in the prophetic books, an independent picture of man. He is a being who is never alone, who, whether he knows it or not, is always and everywhere in continuous partnership with God; he is a being who becomes a person only when he hearkens to the divine address. This is where man is revealed, not in his harmony with the world, but rather always in a situation of extreme jeopardy to himself from the world—how often do the Psalms speak of enemies! But he is also in jeopardy from within himself because of his striving for certainty, by which, as the prophets showed, he most strenuously defends himself against God and flees him. The external physical or political threats and disturbances are not accidental; they are rooted in the disturbance of man's relationship to God. All of this means that man in everything that he does is totally dependent on God and on the approbation—the Old Testament often calls it "grace"—of his creator.

But man, in his incurvate self-interest, cannot know this unaided. It has to be told him in every situation of his life. The pre-exilic prophets in particular seem first of all to embody a single, passionate reaction against all ideals about God to which Israel had become accustomed. By all rhetorical means, that are also quite scandalous, they seek to drag their listeners out of their religious delusion and to give them an unobstructed view of the God to whom one can only hearken—and not after one has secured oneself against God previously by unrefined or refined insurance agreements—the God to whom a man must yield, in whom, in other words, a man must believe. When one reads the prophets, one must always remember that Israel's ancient, sacred language is no longer adequate for truly proper statements about God. They presented the credibility of their God with incredible and audacious words. There was, of course, special reason for the prophets to break the conventional, illusory, and ideal images of God held by their contemporaries, and to unmask their religious activity as profanation of the living God. That witness of the prophets directed the gaze of their contemporaries to the horizon of history and the future. With visions that were sometimes hair-raising in their horror, they let their people see events that would come upon them, events that signified nothing less than the coming of God himself, his self-realization in history and the upheaval in all values that follows from that. They tried in completely untraditional language about God, i.e., by breaking with all language conventions, to direct unobstructed attention to an event that surpasses all human powers of imagination: namely, God's coming, his coming into this human, historical space, his self-realization. The first thing to happen to a man will be a frightful disillusionment. The Tower of Babel, erected by human pride, will collapse, and a gruesome "Twilight of the Idols" will occur.

> The haughty looks of man shall be brought low,
>   and the pride of men shall be humbled;
> and the LORD alone will be exalted in that day.
> For the LORD of hosts has a day
>   against all that is proud and lofty,
>   against all that is lifted up and high;
> against all the cedars of Lebanon,
>   lofty and lifted up;
>   and against all the oaks of Bashan;
> against all the high mountains,
>   and against all the lofty hills;
> against every high tower,
>   and against every fortified wall;
> against all the ships of Tarshish,
>   and against all the beautiful craft.
> And the haughtiness of man shall be humbled,
>   and the pride of men shall be brought low;
>   and the LORD alone will be exalted in that day.
> And the idols shall utterly pass away.
> And men shall enter the caves of the rocks
>   and the holes of the ground,

from before the terror of the LORD,
    and from the glory of his majesty,
    when he rises to terrify the earth.
In that day men will cast forth
    their idols of silver and their idols of gold,
which they made for themselves to worship,
    to the moles and to the bats,
to enter the caverns of the rocks
    and the clefts of the cliffs,
from before the terror of the LORD,
    and from the glory of his majesty,
    when he rises to terrify the earth. (Isa. 2:11-21)

That is the announcement of the great breakdown toward which all history is flowing. But the prophets not only announced it, they were the first to place themselves in this abyss; they were the first to enter this darkness and to descend step by step into an increasingly icy night of judgment. "O that my head were water, and my eyes a fountain of tears" (Jer. 9:1). This breaking of the prophets on God also belongs to the great breakdown toward which the prophets were heading. Jeremiah, of course, bears a double burden, primarily the suffering of his people, but also God's suffering for his people. So far as the latter is concerned, Jeremiah shows us a moving scene. He dictates all these prophecies to his amanuensis, Baruch. But Baruch is unable to stand it any more; it is all beyond his power of endurance. Jeremiah, however, gives him a divine oracle. God says to the amanuensis: "Behold, what I have built I am breaking down, and what I have planted I am plucking up—that is, the whole land. And do you seek great things for yourself? Seek them not; for behold, I am bringing evil upon all flesh, says the Lord; but I will give you your life as a prize of war in all places to which you may go" (Jer. 45:4-5). What that means is that God promises salvation to this man who is condemned to return to dust, all of whose standards for what is great and small are broken, whose idols are demolished. God will begin afresh with him. He will lead Israel into the desert, to the place of her beginning, and there he will allure her and speak tenderly to her (Hos. 2:14). Only through that collapse of the Babylonian tower of human history can God's real work, the *opus proprium* of his love for man, come into view and be revealed. "Lift up your eyes to the heavens, and look at the earth beneath; for the heavens will vanish like smoke, the earth will wear out like a garment, and they who dwell in it will die like gnats; but my salvation will be for ever, and my deliverance will never be ended" (Isa. 51:6). Everything will become new. There will be a new covenant; no one will give thought to the ark of the covenant; and a new servant of God will suffer, more profoundly and beneficially than Moses suffered. The prophet sets the figure of this suffering servant, who is misunderstood by all, over against the whole world of nations precisely at that moment when the world becomes aware that there is something special about this servant of God. God says about him: "Behold, my servant . . . shall be exalted. . . . As many were astonished at him—his appearance was so marred, beyond human semblance, . . . so shall he startle many nations; kings shall shut their mouths because of him; for that which has not been told them they shall see, and that which they have not heard they shall understand" (Isa. 52:13-15). With the message of the prophets the Old Testament opens into a single, extraordinary expectation.

The mystery of Israel—have we at least become aware of it? We certainly have not resolved it. But what Job once said about God is probably also true about this: "Lo, these are but the outskirts of his ways; and how small a whisper do we hear of him!" (26:14). I fear that everything I could say was but a whisper of the mystery of Israel. It certainly must reside in the region of Israel's conversation with God, in God's address to her, in the light of which Israel was revealed to herself, and in the prophetic expectation of God's coming. But is that enough? The early Christian community appealed from the beginning to the Old Testament and its expectations. It thought that Christ could not be understood at all apart from the Old Testament. Is it not true, then, that the Christ who comes is the mystery of Israel? Judaism has contested this interpretation down to the present day. And let us be honest, many Christians today are also unable to understand the Old Testament in that way. There remains for us, therefore, only this: to wrestle further to understand the Old Testament; for it is clear that this book is a stone of testing and a book of destiny for all mankind.

11

THE BIBLICAL STORY OF CREATION

(Lecture on South German radio in the series "Belief in Creation and the Theory of Evolution." First published in Kröners Pocketbook edition, vol. 230, 1955, pp. 25-37, A. Kröner Verlag, Stuttgart.)

For many centuries the biblical story of creation was absolutely authoritative for faith and knowledge in all of Christendom. No one doubted either that God had created the world and held it ever since in his almighty power or that he had created it in the way described in the book of Genesis. This uncritical confidence in the creation story's reliability even for natural science, as we said, has begun to disintegrate in our time. Herder considered the Old Testament to be the oldest document of mankind, but his viewpoint is unmistakably altered. The creation story is indeed a human document. No one in his time praised it more than Herder did, but as a human document, one among others. The nadir in this disappearance of confidence in the creation story was reached in the Babel-Bible debate at the beginning of our century. That was a debate in which the Assyriologist Friedrich Delitzsch of Berlin maintained the priority and the unconditional and qualitative precedence of the Babylonian creation stories over against the biblical report of creation. The Old Testament was simply included among the great number of documents in the history of religions, and after that it was only a question of literary, aesthetic, and religious taste as to which document appealed more to the reader. As an enlightened European one kept one's distance, in effect, from all of them.

In this brief article I cannot, of course, succeed in clearing up all questions, least of all questions of faith. Much would be gained, however, if these few pages could contribute something to a better understanding of the first chapter of the Bible, and if they could succeed in showing briefly how we today see this text scientifically and theologically. In that respect, one must first remember that this text does not simply stand on its own, that is, it is not a self-contained document that could be interpreted completely by itself. No, the report about creation is only the beginning of an enormous book. This book is a history; it begins with the creation of the world, leads to the history of the patriarchs and to the nation, Israel. It pauses for a while with the events at Mt. Sinai and ends with Israel's settlement in the promised land of Canaan. Scholars call it the *Hexateuch,* for it encompasses the narrative history of the five books of Moses and the book of Joshua. We should not, however, imagine it to be like a modern book with one author and a year of publication. Israel was writing this book over four hundred years. Nevertheless, this book is not a coral reef of haphazardly assembled literature. It has, rather, a clear arrangement and also an exciting plot. It shows how Israel came into existence, how God directed her history, and what universal plans God had for her. What is strange, however, is that this book, Israel's great etiology, does not begin as one might expect it would with Abraham, the first patriarch of the early period, but rather with the creation of the world. That, of course, encompasses an enormous claim: to speak properly about Israel, to understand Israel correctly, one must begin with the creation of the world; for Israel has its place in God's plans for the world. It is for that reason that the book of Genesis begins with the creation. The creation story is not told out of what might be called a neutral, scientific interest in the question about the origin of the world, as ancient Greek natural philosophy searched for an ultimate principle on the basis of which this world might be comprehended. Rather, the story is told because here a history began, a history between God and man, in which Israel was to receive a central position. That is the meaning of the beginning of the Bible. One misunderstands Israel, her faith and her worship, unless one sees it all from the vantage point of the creation of the world. Only from that perspective are the things that this book says about Israel placed in proper proportion.

What I have intended to point out is where in Israel interest in creation arose. It sounds paradoxical, but it is appropriate to say that Israel was interested in creation not because of nature and its problems, but because of history.

As we turn, then, to the old text and some details that have been interpreted so many times before, we will begin with a prior consideration: how may it have originated? Everything speaks against such a chapter as the biblical creation story having originated in the kind of an individual who could have written it down at a certain time. Declarations of such breadth and claim to value about God and the world, and about God and man, did not arise in antiquity in the enlightened individual mind. Indeed, according to the view of the ancients, no individual could justify the claim to attention which those declarations made. They were doctrine; i.e., they were traditions of the priests. Doctrine means, furthermore, that they were very carefully considered by the priests, passed on from generation to generation, and constantly purified of everything that did not accord with Israel's faith. One can say, therefore, that the theological and cosmological thought of Israel had been at work on this chapter for centuries. It follows that the language of this report about creation is very compact and highly precise. Everything that is said here is to be accepted exactly as it is written; nothing is to be interpreted symbolically or metaphorically. The language is actually scientific, though not in the modern sense of the word.

That is to say, it is freed from ornamentation and poetic emotion and is factual to the point of monotony, a monotony and a concentration whose effect, to be sure, is monumental. Anyone who reads aloud only the beginning senses that. "In the beginning God created the heavens and the earth. The earth was without form and void, and darkness was upon the face of the deep; and the Spirit of God was moving over the face of the waters. And God said, 'Let there be light'; and there was light" (Gen. 1:1-3).

One must try to put aside all familiarity with the opening statements in order to see their grandeur afresh. Let us try for a moment to do that by establishing what they do not say. The majority of all creation myths begin with a creative struggle among the mythically personified, elemental forces, usually between two original principals, one light and good, the other dark and evil. Instead of that, the biblical account speaks of God, who existed before the world, who freely created the world, and who is therefore its lord. His creation came about through his creative word alone. Again let me explain first what is not meant by that and what misconception is being thereby prevented. Almost all theories of creation in the religions of the world are emanative, i.e., they understand the world not so much as the god's creation as they do an effluence, an emanation of the god's essence. But that conception erases the boundary between God and world. The world becomes, in a sense, another manifestation or self-representation of the god. When Israel, in contrast to that, says that God created the world by his word, she expresses not only the complete effortlessness of creation but also an absolutely essential distance between Creator and creature. The world does not partake of deity as the emanation of a god, but it is creature and as such has its own glory. This opening sentence is in a way the sum of the whole creation account, and it is developed step by step in the following verses.

It has often been cause for surprise that the second

statement of the account of creation mentions chaos, i.e., the state of affairs before creation. This chaos is defined as watery, dark, and abysmal. But what sense is there in defining chaos so precisely once creation has already been mentioned previously? Does not the creation story revert in its second verse to a stage before the grandiose position which the first verse occupied in its sharp rise of enthusiasm? The matter must be explained to mean that the conception of creation, as the report intends it, cannot be rightly grasped or thought unless it is contrasted with chaos, the unformed mass that existed before the world began. Chaos is man's primeval experience. We meet it daily and are affrighted by it; for all creation is threatened by chaos and can revert to the abyss of the formless at any moment. Our story of creation tells us that creation means not only that God called this world into being at the beginning, but that he continually preserves and sustains all creation from the abyss of the formless by which it is threatened every second. One should not be deceived by the stony immobility of the objective, written report. The matters which are mentioned are permeated by powerful, inner tensions. Think only of the creation of day and night that now occurs. God has let light into the abysmal night of chaos. From the indescribable mixture that thereupon ensues, and we have to understand all of that quite realistically, God lifts out the element of light and creates day. The origin of light is something quite different. Night is in a sense a vestige of the darkness of chaos that has now been incorporated into a beneficial, creative order. That too is a primeval, human experience. Every night brings something of the absolute darkness of chaos to the earth; every night dissolves the contours of creation into formlessness. And every morning is a kind of new creation, as its light again lifts creation out of formless darkness. The uneducated person greets the night with dread; it is a threat to creation and also to his personal existence. Our familiar, evening hymns of the church bear witness to this fear of the night.

The divergence of the following verses (6-10) from our conceptions of natural science appears particularly great. The entire, ancient Near East considered the celestial sphere that covers the disk of the earth to be a massive heavenly body, i.e., an enormous, stable, heavenly bell. Our word, "firmament," i.e., solidity, derives from that conception. Luther, in his translation, speaks of "the solidity." The disk of the earth and its heavenly, ball-like covering comprise the basic framework of the universe. Now follows the creation of plants (vv. 11-13). But here the language of the creation story changes. God does not say, "Let there be plants," but "Let the earth put forth vegetation." In other words God summons and empowers the earth to participate independently in the work of creation. The term, *natura,* here emerges as independent, creative nature. She is, to be sure, greatly circumscribed by the preceding divine commission and authorization. Actually the plants are dependent directly on the earth alone; they sprout from it and they return to it again.

For the creation of the constellations to follow that of the plants will not at all conform with our view of the world (vv. 14-19). The text seems to presume an original light that was present at first before the light of the stars came into being; actually the creation of light took place long before that of the stars. But apart from this special problem, the paragraph about the creation of the constellations is one of the most astonishing in our creation story. One has to remember that it arose in a time and environment that were fully devoted to the cult of the stars, i.e., that considered the stars to be divine beings. And now let the cool sobriety with which the stars are referred to as creatures and heavenly bodies have its effect: "And God said, 'Let there be lights in the firmament of the heavens to separate the day from the night; and let them be for signs and for seasons and for days and years!' " Let one apprehend the serviceable function here accorded the constellations in the makeup of the world. In these statements too, which are so calmly written down, there lives a powerful, antimythical passion.

After this comes the report of the creation of fish, birds, and beasts of the earth. But we turn immediately to what was from the start the goal and climax of the whole creation story, the creation of man (vv. 26-30). Here one can see especially well the minor interest this creation story has in all natural science. It is interested not in understanding nature itself but rather, from paragraph to paragraph, in its relation to God, i.e., in the problem of faith. It is not difficult to see, indeed, that this story of creation is a confession, in spite of its restrained language. I just said that it is interested in the relation of things to God, and it becomes immediately clear that very striking distinctions are made in details. Most distant from God is the dimension of the chaotic; we have spoken about the created difference between day and night and also about the plants having their direct dependence on the earth. The same thing is true for the animals; but they are singled out over the plants in one decisive point, for God blessed them, i.e., he gave them the fruitfulness to multiply on their own. We have, therefore, an ascending line; at the tip of the pyramid is man, for he alone of all creatures is the closest to God. His creation alone is preceded by a solemn decision in God's heart: "Let us make man in our image." Only man, therefore, owes his existence to a voluntary decision in the depths of God's heart. Furthermore, God took the model for man from the upper world and created man in the divine image. Indeed, he established man as his own governor on earth. Man is to represent in his rule God's claim to lordship on earth. Every relationship to God in the world is thus summed up in man. In him the world has its most direct connection to God; no creature is closer to God than he. Before God he is the center and goal of creation. Obviously these are not the declarations of natural science; they are confessions of faith of the most compact kind.

Oddly, this report of creation does not conclude with

man's creation. At its end it returns again to God and touches on the innermost mystery of the creator and his creation, on God's rest. This rest is not, of course, what one might call a private matter for God alone; rather, our text understands it as a side of God turned to the world. God, the text says, has blessed this rest. It is mentioned almost as an object between God and the world. It has often been said that this passage refers to the inauguration of the sabbath. But stated in that way it is not true, for what is mentioned here is a rest that has long been present, before man was ordered to observe it and bind his life to it. At creation God designed this world for rest. This declaration, like everything in this chapter, is formulated with extreme density; it is not written for edifying reading but as a distillation of theological doctrine. This statement in particular, that the Creator of the world designed the world for rest, that a promise of rest has hung over it since creation, should now be interpreted from a great variety of viewpoints.

But we cannot indulge in such thoughts here; rather, we must once more turn in conclusion to the story of creation as whole. As we have seen, it is a thoroughly theological document. It does not talk of the world and its natural problems as such, but rather of God. God created, God spoke, God saw, God separated, God set, God finished, God blessed. It is concerned with matters of faith, matters to be believed. One should consider especially the concluding statement that rounds off the account: "God saw everything that he had made, and behold, it was very good." This "very good" could be translated better as "fully complete." That is to say, everything had come into being exactly as God had planned it. So far as that is concerned, no incompleteness attaches to the creation. Nothing evil has been put in it by God. Ponder what that means: this judgment is passed on our world, a world of the most varied riddles and dissonances. In this respect there can be no doubt about the intention of the biblical story of creation; it is intended as theological doctrine.

On the other hand, there is more than a little natural science in the chapter. It would be unfair to deny that the ancients had a science, that they struggled earnestly to understand the world and its parts and that they arrived at quite definite perceptions and distinctions. They classified plants, for example, into those that cast seed directly and those whose seed is contained in their fruit; they distinguished among the animals; and in its chronology of the primeval period, the creation story simply follows the scientific theory of its time. Christians have had to learn, amid severe shocks to their faith, that this view of the world is quite antiquated.

If the report of creation had been limited to saying that in the beginning God created the world, if it had been satisfied with the confession of the first verse, then we would have been spared all challenges on this point. But just as faith makes individual declarations about God's relationship to the creatures and their relationship to one another, so it must speak here and there about matters as it perceives them from the scientific viewpoint of its time. We would have to do the same thing. We do occasionally have to express our faith with the help of our current understanding of nature. The fact that the scientific world view of Genesis 1 is no longer ours is established, and the file about it is closed. To be sure, we are reminded occasionally that this account of creation does seem to coincide with certain perceptions of more recent natural science, especially in the successive sequence of plants, animals, and man. Now it is quite possible that the natural science of that ancient time had reached some conclusions that our modern, rational, natural science has also reached in quite different ways. One must remember, of course, that those men of antiquity acquired their knowledge of the world quite differently, for when looking at nature they made use not only of pure reason but also in a certain sense of "vision." They had a "sense apparatus" and had at their disposal meditative possibilities that perhaps were at certain points superior to our thoroughly rationalized mentality. Nevertheless, however interesting such facts may be, it would be absurd to try to support the biblical account of creation with such arguments to back up its scientific conclusions. Its science is absolutely outdated.

In spite of that, the story does show us something extremely important about the relationship of faith to science. It shows us that we cannot simply modernize the story by replacing the ancient, outmoded science with modern conclusions about nature. That is connected with the fact that in this story theological and scientific knowledge are intertwined in an extraordinary fashion. Both sets of statements, the theological and the scientific, are not only parallel but intertwined in such a way that one cannot say at any point that a sentence is scientific, and therefore not applicable to us, or that it is purely theological, and therefore still relevant for faith. Theology found in the science of that time an instrument it could use unhesitatingly to unfold the content of faith. One could speak of the very same matter theologically or scientifically. We find that particularly difficult these days because our modern science is no longer open to the world of faith, and because it formulates its conclusions so much on the basis of a concealed dogmatism that it blocks the way to a statement of faith about the same subject of investigation. As we have said, our account of creation, with respect to its knowledge of nature, shares in the prevailing conceptions of the ancient Near East. So far as its specific content is concerned, however, it is far removed from contemporary myths of creation. What it has in common with the myths of neighboring peoples is scarcely more than a few basic, cosmological ideas and terms. What is decisive is that these terms, e.g., *tehom* for the abyss of chaos, have been divested of their mythical content in the biblical story of creation and are used simply as technical terms in the priestly cosmology.

We saw at the beginning that our account of creation is only the beginning of a historical work. With this account of the creation of the world there is also sketched the plan of history, and in fact of a single history in which God's saving acts are revealed in ascending measure. The enthusiastic hymns of the Psalter agree fully with this more reserved, priestly doctrine when they praise the creation of the world as God's first saving act.

12

THE REALITY OF GOD

(Concluding lecture at the church conference in Hamburg, April 1958. First published in Reality Today, *"Papers and reports of the church conference in Hamburg," edited by Hans Hermann Walz, 1958, pp. 89-105, Kreuz-Verlag, Stuttgart.)*

People react these days to the question about God's reality in two ways. For the person, especially the intellectual person who is most actively engaged in finding out more about himself and his world, the question appears very disturbing. He scarcely knows who he is; how is he to know who God is? Cannot this question be left alone or put off or understood as the hobby of a religiously engaged group?

> Beyond, for us, the view is barred.
> The Fool, who gazes blinking yonder
> Sees himself in every cloud;
> Let him stand and look about him here.
> This world reveals its secrets to the diligent.
> What need has he to roam about eternity?
> Let him grasp the facts of earth.

That is without question a very manly and also sufficiently modern sentiment, and we know only too well that those who by contrast talk so much about God often do not cut a good figure. But what if the question about God is not about something "yonder" but about something here? At any rate, there is another group opposed to this one, a group of those who know or cannot get free from the fact that all our striving is from start to finish lost effort, if we do not understand ourselves in the light of God. They think it is simply an illusion to consider man as the established and given fact and God as the doubtful one. On the contrary, man is man only before God and with God; and wherever he loses this connection, he becomes immediately and without fail a monster. For a life without God is a life that God no longer defends. Rest for that soul, or in more modern terms a feeling of security in this world, cannot be found except in God.

It is not my task here to argue the reasons for this point of view. I would like in this company to proceed on the assumption that we have assembled because most of us belong to the second group. But I have to make one reservation. Those who entrusted this lecture to me gave me permission to speak particularly about that to which my life's work has been dedicated, the Old Testament. I have accepted this permission in good conscience, because it has long since become clear that the great disorder, not to say chaos, in Christian conceptions derives essentially from the fact that the Old Testament has ceased to speak to us. What then does this Old Testament show us? It shows us one people like many others, but one people that was unceasingly occupied with the word of God. They were occupied, to be sure, not always to their own glory, often denying it or even rejecting it, but still in a living relationship, kept alive by this God. And they developed more and more profoundly a singular knowledge of God and his way of speaking, so that one of them could one day pray, "My rock, be not deaf to me, lest, if thou be silent to me, I become like those who go down to the Pit" (Ps. 28:1). Here the author sees clearly that when God is silent, man wastes away and cannot recover from his disorders.

Now because Israel was so knowledgeable about matters between God and man, we can expect her to help us understand the question we have posed. Before we seek the answer, it is well to consider how the question about God's reality could be taken and, from the human standpoint, what all, even the faint overtones, is involved in it. It happens that this very question arises in the Bible at the time when God called Moses to tell Israel that he, God, was preparing to rescue his people. Moses, however, did not go quietly and obediently. Rather he stopped and asked God a counter question. It is as though he said, "Lord, that will not do. The matter is not so simple, for if I should go now they would ask me at once, 'Who is this God of whom you speak? What is his name?' And what am I then to say?" (Exod. 3:13).

This little interlude, this rather disturbing objection that Moses makes, is extraordinarily interesting, and much depends on our understanding correctly what Moses was looking for in answer to his question. What does this question about God's name mean? It is certainly much more than the search for a term, for a divine epithet. In contrast to men of the modern west, those men were firmly convinced that their lives were on every side supported, surrounded, and permeated by divine powers, that they lived with a continuous influence of the metaphysical, that they were unable to disentangle themselves from these powers. A man was at the mercy of these powers, and that means that basically he had to suffer from them more than be helped or blessed by them. Thus what Moses expected from his people (if we may trivialize it somewhat) was, "We have no interest in a new God, in your augmenting the history of religion by the addition of one God; in any event, not so long as we do not know precisely what is involved."

Now I think this is the question of people who want to come to the point in religion. To be sure it is a question which arises from profound religious disillusionment; it is a question refined of all vestiges of religious sentimentality; it raises coolly and soberly the matter of God's reality and its meaning for man. If we want to illuminate the question psychologically, we cannot avoid noting the presence of an irreverent audacity; I mean that audacity, which, when it has tested an approach and found it adequate, will not hesitate to use it. And this taking hold, this primeval human drive to place God in one's service—in ancient times one must consider the possibility of magic; in modern times there are equivalent possibilities—is something frightful; for wherever one poses the question about God's reality, there is also this hand that would like to bind God so that he is always visible. In that night when Jacob wrestled with God, face to face the narrator tells us, he too asked about God's name: "What is your name?" . . . But the man answered him, "Why is it that you ask my name?" "And there he blessed him. . . . The sun rose upon Jacob as he passed Penuel" (Gen. 32:24-30). From that we can learn, evidently, that man, even when he is wrestled by God to the dust, will still have this question always on his lips, this question in which is expressed man's whole religious need as well as all his audacity in the face of God. All of that is contained in the question man asks about the reality of God. There is no basis for the optimistic assumption that the question as we pose it today is any different. The answer God gave to Moses reads, when properly translated: "I will be present as I will be present." One who hears this statement will not immediately succeed in comprehending its content and inner range. It sounds like a promise but also has traces of an abrupt evasion. The promise of God's presence, or as Buber thinks God's faithfulness, is indeed here, but at the same time, in the paronomastic conclusion, one perceives how God, precisely in his existence for man, intends to guard his freedom. This statement, to be sure, is somewhat isolated in the Old Testament, for ancient Israel was not accustomed to formulate sharp paradoxes regarding ultimate matters between God and man. I too do not want to discuss God's statement further, for one reason, because our readiness to expect real help and benefit from such theological paradoxes is small. How much of her experience with God Israel packed into this statement can best be known at the end of this lecture. We will, for the time being then, quietly take our eyes from it. It is enough for us to see that Israel at that time entrusted herself to this God who had introduced himself to her so strangely. She did so, to be sure, with hesitation, full of reservations and with avenues of retreat left open. She did so with the same unsuspecting attitude of those who today entrust themselves to God, who also do not know that with the first word God has spoken over them a decision has been made that cannot be retracted for all eternity. Even deep in the desert, when the spies returned from the Promised Land, Israel thought she was free before God to liquidate her history with him and return again to Egypt (Num. 14:1 ff.). But that is the way of men with God. God's redeemed people was a shilly-shallying, rebellious crowd!

And yet, consider everything that happened to this people! How it handled everything, by God and through God, about itself and the world! It is indeed remarkable that when we want to speak of God's reality we need not put everything earthly behind us or strain to rise to a pure view of God, but rather that we need to speak about man as he stands revealed before God, and about the world as it can be known only to one who knows about the living God. We have to proceed in this way because God, with his words and acts, has entered the world of this man. Because of that Israel knew that God was present, and because of that her certainty could not be shaken, even when at times the image of God was distorted for her, when it assumed frightful and incomprehensible characteristics. Men of today, when they no longer understand God, say "No, there is no God." The ancients would presumably have called that a very naive deduction. For Job the incomprehensible God, who threatened him on every side, was still no less real. Everything suggests that he was much more real to him as he says significantly at the end of the book than the God he had known only by hearsay (Job 42:5). Whether there is a God receives no discussion at all in the Bible.

There is only one question, whether you can say to him: "thou art with me; thy rod and thy staff, they comfort me" (Ps. 23:4); or whether you cry out to him with Job: "How long wilt thou not look away from me, nor let me alone till I swallow my spittle?" (Job 7:19). Those are the only human alternatives in the presence of God's reality.

But do not expect me now to speak of the judgment and grace of God as they are in fact overwhelmingly attested by the Psalms and Prophets. I will not do that, because I am afraid that it will all be understood too quickly in terms of the traditional notions of our personal, introspective Christianity. I want to begin at a quite different point, namely, with the biblical struggle against other gods. What is particularly important about that? We will not waste any words showing that it has to do with something much more than an enlightened reduction of the pantheon to a single God, i.e., something other than a self-evident truth. If the struggle were only that, then all we would have to explain would be Israel's protection of the first commandment with an intolerance that would not be humanized, with an almost frantic intolerance that did not shrink before any affront. Here we evidently have a parting of intellectual ways. Must we, in the interest of a purer view of God, keep our distance from this struggle against the gods, this contest which at times obsessed the people of Israel? Many today think we must. Intellectuals in particular have uncomfortable feelings about this struggle. Or do we here stand at the door of the biblical knowledge of God without which everything else we think we have understood is nothing? "I am the Lord your God. You shall have no other gods before me." "You shall not make for youself a graven image, or any likeness of anything that is in heaven above, or that is in the earth beneath, or that is in the water under the earth; you shall not bow down to them or serve them."

In this contest against other gods and against images we must understand quite clearly that what is here pointed out is the danger, the Bible calls it an absolutely deadly delusion for man, that stands in the way of every

113

perception of the true God and every life with him. Let us call it the myth, i.e., that enigmatic and creative ability man has to objectify and to deify certain primeval experiences or events which he has encountered in his sphere of existence. We are using the risky and ambiguous term, "myth," in the sense of a reaction that innate thought has to the powers that determine our life. These powers, however, which include the established orders, are finite. Man, of course, does not know that. He projects them in various distortions into the realm of the metaphysical and regards them as divine. Think of the divinization of the heavenly bodies, the dying and awakening of nature that has been reified in heavenly persons, the mystery of procreation that was envisaged as divine in Canaan in the image of the bull. We will mention more recent practices in a moment. It is always the same: man says "gods," but he means the abyss of the world. Myths are symbols for the world with which men of antiquity and more clear-headed men of today form their understanding of the world, and they do so with images in which their experience becomes solid. The myth is essentially thought in symbols, and since man continues to encounter new mysteries he must continue to erect new altars and institute new mythical symbolizations. And that is what the Bible considers monstrous, this knowledge about the wall of images that separates man from God. Israel's solitariness in the world of religions was that she knew about idols and idolatry. She was not, of course, in the superior position of one who knows better. She had again and again to extricate herself from the overpowering temptation to worship idols and images, and she was often enough overpowered by their embrace. We see the prophets incessantly occupied with breaking down for their people the idolatrous images of the devout person who is most tempted to make God in his own or another image. And the prophets exhausted themselves in this struggle for the simple reason that man is lost whenever he trusts the "nothings," as the Bible calls them, and so loses God. It is a decision between God and nothingness. But as Israel learned that man himself erects these images and forms gods for himself, she was able on occasion to break out in pious laughter at this zeal for idol-building and at the dance peoples indulge in before the gods they had themselves manufactured. Consider, for example, second Isaiah's satirical tractate on idol-making:

> [The carpenter] cuts down cedars. . . . Then it becomes fuel for a man; he takes a part of it and warms himself, he kindles a fire and bakes bread; also he makes a god and worships it, he makes it a graven image and falls down before it. Half of it he burns in the fire . . . he roasts meat and is satisfied; also he warms himself and says, "Aha, I am warm. . . ." And the rest of it he makes into a god, his idol; and falls down to it and worships it; he prays to it and says, "Deliver me, for thou art my god!" (Isa. 44:14-17)

We can thus say with assurance that the first and second commandments concern the question of whether God is appearance or reality. But if I am to clarify for you this struggle of Israel against the persistent mythicizing of the world and God himself, I have to overcome a difficulty. I said that the mysteries and unfathomable powers that can break out in our sphere of life are not always the same; they change their appearance. We are no longer tempted today to conjure with dark powers of the earth as men of the Middle Ages did. And no one today has a trace of that drive to assign divine rank to the stars. We can no longer imagine the strength of forbearance that was once required, as for Job, not to grant the moon "moving in splendor" any cultic reverence and to refrain from throwing it a kiss (Job 31:26-27). If I were now to speak topically and not only historically, I would have to mention powers and magnitudes that play almost the same role for us today and have for us mythical dignity. They present a kind of iconostasis that must be broken down if we want to know the reality of God. I will mention two conceptions that at first seem harmless enough because the whole world uses them, whether thoughtfully or thoughtlessly. I refer to the terms "nature" and "history." Now of course they are not gods in the sense of the word as it is used in the phenomenology of religion. Nevertheless, one must ask whether the absolute quality they have for us does not fill the position which in antiquity was filled by gods or at least by myths. We just said that the ancients' perception of the world happened in myths; and in fact an inclination toward mythical dogmatism is latent in all modern science too. In C. F. von Weizsäcker's *History of Nature* we read that "the idea of unending Nature, existing by itself . . . is the myth of modern science. Science, which began by destroying the myth of the Middle Ages, is now forced by being consistent to the knowledge that it has substituted another myth in its place." What Weizsäcker says here about the concept, nature, can also be said in analagous fashion about the concept, history. We have absolutized both conceptions in such a way that we can incorporate them into Christian faith only with difficulty. Let me attempt, using the Bible, to show you what could happen if we were able to destroy this iconostasis which we have burdened with the concepts of nature and history.

Israel was not familiar with the concept of nature, nor did she speak about the world as a cosmos, i.e., about an ordered structure that is self-contained and subject to definite laws. To her the world was primarily much more an event than a being, and certainly much more a personal experience than a neutral subject for investigation. But we can never express it satisfactorily. For Israel the world was, to formulate it somewhat epigrammatically, an unceasing, supporting, ordering activity of God. But it was not, in the sense Goethe imagined, a self-representation or an emanation streaming of itself from God, which therefore increased the impression in the world of experiences of the incalculable and the mysterious. "Thou dost beset me behind and before. . . . Such knowledge is too wonderful for me; . . . I cannot attain it" (Ps. 139:5-6). Let me show that by bringing together two very striking texts. The well-known Psalm 104 speaks about the world's being threatened by the chaotic dimension of primeval waters from which it is protected by God's will for order. God, it says, has beneficially incorporated these chaotic waters into creation, so that they provide for the creatures in the form of springs and brooks. Thus there is water for plants and trees, there are trees for the birds, mountains for the badgers, constellations for the seasons, and nights for beasts of prey. According to this psalm the world is a single, ordered structure that is governed by God; it is not a self-contained cosmos, for the key to the entire psalm is the statement: "These all look to thee, to give them their food in due season. When thou givest to them, they gather it up; when thou openest thy hand, they are filled with good things. When thou hidest thy face, they are dismayed, . . . and return to their dust" (Ps. 104:27-29). Here the world is not seen as "nature," but rather as lying before God, waiting before him, completely open. In that moment it needs his blessing and grace, and thanks be to God it shares unceasingly in his blessing.

I must add a brief word about this blessing that permeates the world, as Israel perceived it in faith, and about the praise that goes forth from this creation and precisely from those realms that are far from men, namely, from the deserts and from distant peoples, and even from the animal world. We are concerned here with what we call "beauty." While beauty is for us only one part of the iconostasis, the Bible sees it not as existing for itself, or self-contained, but rather as a reflection of the divine glory. We are concerned with a *doxa* that is poured out over creation and returns to God in immense excitement. "All thy works shall give thanks to thee" says Psalm 145:10, and it is interesting that the Hebrew word for "give thanks" also means "confess." "All thy works shall confess thee!" That is what I meant when I spoke of this excitement of returning the splendor. "Let the desert and its cities lift up their voice, the villages that Kedar inhabits; let the inhabitants of Sela sing for joy, let them shout from the top of the mountains" (Isa. 42:11).

Above all, we have to read the great concluding speech in the book of Job, which wants to show how everything in this world is glorious, uselessly glorious. Special are the charming miniatures of animals: the wild horse that frisks far from all human advantage; behemoth, which you cannot tether for your sweetheart; and the ostrich, to which God gave "no share in understanding." Everything about this bird seems shameful, her wings, her rearing of young, and the way she treats her eggs, but if anyone wants to hunt her, "she laughs at the horse and his rider" (Job 39; 40:15-24).

That is a world at the laying of whose foundation stone the heavenly choirs sang for joy. Therefore the rebellious Job had to be asked, "Where were you when I laid the foundation of the earth? . . . when the morning stars sang together, and all the sons of God shouted for joy?" (Job 38:4-7).

But if we had easily considered all this, we would still have to cite again the author of the book of Job: "Lo, these are but the outskirts of his ways; and how small a whisper do we hear of him! But the thunder of his power who can understand?" (Job 26:14).

I have said that Psalm 104 pictures the world as it lies before God. But how about as it lies before man? In the book of Job there is an extraordinary poem that stands relatively alone. It begins with a description of mining operations to show something of the astounding technical potentialities men have. What bounds then are set to his aspiration? He burrows under mountains and brings to light metals from the depths of the earth; men hang on ropes in mine-shafts. But the most important thing he seeks he cannot find: "But where shall wisdom be found?" By wisdom the poem understands that indescribable, undefinable something, that innermost mystery that God implanted in creation, perhaps that which we are accustomed to call its "meaning." About this mystery of the world, about this wisdom, man has to say: "It is hid from the eyes of all living, . . . Abaddon and Death say, 'We have heard a rumor of it with our ears.' God understands the way to it. . . . For he looks to the ends of the earth" (Job 28). From here then, and that is a final word of the Bible, no way leads to God. He is too deeply hidden in his creation. The preacher of Ecclesiastes says with similar meaning: "As you do not know how the bones grow in the womb of a woman with child, so you do not know the work of God who makes everything" (11:5). "However much man may toil in seeking, he will not find it out; even though a wise man claims to know, he cannot find it out" (8:17).

We said that the ancients did not know the concept of nature; so now we must answer the question about what it was they saw opposing themselves, those who were not in a position to conjure and objectify their environment with such a magical formula or let what they regarded as an event, a personal experience, congeal, so to speak, in a neutral concept. I fear that it was something very much more overwhelming and, to be theological, something very much more unfathomable than we can today imagine; it was something that one can in fact endure only in the upward look to God the Creator.

And now to that which we call history! "In that day the Lord will whistle for the fly which is at the sources of the streams of Egypt, and for the bee which is in the land of Assyria. . . . In that day the Lord will shave with a razor which is hired beyond the [Euphrates] River . . . the head and the hair of the feet and it will sweep away the beard also" (Isa. 7:18-20). Isaiah said that to his Judaean contemporaries; for him God could summon the world empires as one whistles for animals; he saw God as a barber who borrowed for his razor a world empire! Israel had a cultic language, words about God that had been shaped by centuries of reverent speaking, unchanged and unchangeable for millennia. When God commanded it, however, one could speak, breaking every pious convention and apparently without any feeling for dignity and manners. (That too seems to me to belong in the chapter on the reality of God, namely, his reality in the medium of language.) Consider the monstrous word that God spoke through the mouth of the prophet Hosea: "Therefore I am like a moth* to Ephraim, and like dry rot to the house of

Judah" (5:12). (*Although thus in all recent translations, it seems probable that the word usually translated "moth" should be rendered "rottenness.") The prophet's contemporaries would perhaps have conceded that the people were afflicted wih social, political, or economic ills. But Hosea meant something quite different: the people are afflicted with God. "When Ephraim saw his sickness, and Judah his wound, then Ephraim went to Assyria, and sent to the great king. But he is not able to cure you or heal your wound" (Hosea 5:13).

These prophets seem to have inverted all relationships. They do not seem to have seen at all the great problems with which their age struggled, especially the political problem of securing the state. Instead they see God approaching them with a magnitude and directness of which none of their contemporaries knew anything. For it is true that when a threatening empire moves into our range of vision it fills all historical space, and God, who is at work in the background, appears only shadowlike to men. But the prophet does not permit the very imposing historical phenomena to distract his gaze from God. That empire on the Tigris river is a borrowed razor; it seems to have no power of its own at all. All activity proceeds from God. We may call this realm history; it is in any case clasped entirely by God's hands. But man's inability to see that constituted the prophetic suffering. When Sennacherib in 701 B.C. marched against Jerusalem, his advance unleashed feverish activity in the threatened city; and when it was all over, Isaiah denounced his contemporaries: "You saw that the breaches of the city of David were many, and you collected the waters of the lower pool, . . . and you broke down the houses to fortify the wall. . . . But you did not look to him who did it, or have regard for him who planned it long ago" (Isa. 22:9-11).

But what could they have seen, because of course it was not the same thing every time. Isaiah means to say that they could have found their security in God. If you were to succeed in taking shelter in the event that has now come upon you, if you were to succeed in pulling yourselves together and entrusting yourselves to this divine future, then you would be saved. That would be faith. For you, faith would mean giving space to God and his rule and not letting human intrigues usurp his place. But at other times the message was different. Above all their particular contents, however, is nevertheless the one word, breakdown—the breakdown toward which history streams, the breakdown of their towers of Babylon and their false altars. And that happens because nations are approaching an ultimate revelation, a self-revelation of God in history. Then, not only God will be revealed, but man too; and the impotence of that to which he has clung previously will also be revealed. The passage in Isaiah where the prophetic prediction mentions the great twilight of the idols that will come to pass "on that day," is of overpowering grandeur.

> And the idols shall utterly pass away. . . . In that day men will cast forth their idols of silver and their idols of gold, which they made for themselves to worship, to the moles and to the bats, to enter the caverns of the rocks and the clefts of the cliffs, from before the terror of the Lord, and from the glory of his majesty, when he rises to terrify the earth. (Isa. 2:18-21)

The poem is in the form of a hymn; there is joy in it. This is the way the prophet looks forward to God's self-realization in history. But such a delight may have been granted these men only on momentary occasions. In the foreground was their struggle with their contemporaries who had long since emancipated themselves from any serious faith. I have already said that the prophets struggled to destroy their false certainties and to rescue these men from the matted mass of safeguards with which they had supplied themselves as in a house. Zephaniah formulated it once in a divine oracle: "At that time I will search Jerusalem with lamps, and I will punish the men who are thickening upon their lees" (Zeph. 1:12).

Here the reality of God is indeed quite directly the subject of these prophetic words. One thing, however, has to be said clearly if the prophets are not to be misunderstood. God, who whistles for an empire to come, who as barber borrows a knife, who lodges in Israel's joints as a disease, who shines light into the corners of houses—all of that means that God is hidden; it all means that God does not reveal himself in his glory, but that he does his work in strange self-effacement and prepares history for his coming. Indeed, "Behold, the nations are like a drop from a bucket, and are accounted as the dust on the scales" (Isa. 40:15). But that is only one verse; another says, "The Lord will rise up . . . to do his deed—strange is his deed! and to work his work—alien is his work!" (Isa. 28:21).

But let no one think that the prophets looked with arms folded at this on-going drama of the breakdown of history and the revelation of human nature or that they resigned themselves in philosophical calmness to the inevitable. They were the first to enter into this breakdown and to be overwhelmed by its terrors and temptations. As the first, they advanced to meet the God who kept concealing himself more and more; step by step they descended into God-forsakenness and entered that realm of extreme outer darkness into which the Evangelist says that Jesus went on the night in which he was betrayed. Only from afar can we in imagination accompany Jeremiah on this path into the final night:

> "The harvest is past, the summer is ended, and we are not saved." For the wound of the daughter of my people is my heart wounded, I mourn, and dismay has taken hold on me. Is there no balm in Gilead? Is there no physician there? Why then has the health of the daughter of my people not been restored? O that my head were waters, and my eyes a fountain of tears. (Jer. 8:20–9:1)

And when Jeremiah said that, he was far from the last stage of his life that was finally shattered on the hiddenness of God. Some psalm writers too reached the vicinity of this outermost dimension of God-forsakenness, where horror had to choke every attempt they made to find meaning.

Let us be thankful that all of that has been preserved, that it has not been explained away, and above all that it has not been profoundly mythicized, in the sense, e.g., of a cosmic dualism. These men at prayer could do only one thing: they directed this realm of outermost darkness to God. On this point we may not neglect to mention the passion of Jesus, which our dogmatic theologians call the work of Christ and about which a passion hymn says that Jesus went "to the world's night to do the work that sets us right." For here we have only to do with the conquest of this extreme outer darkness. But there is a text in the Old Testament that reaches beyond the humiliation of our Lord. It aims at the moment when God will present the suffering servant of God to the entire world, toward that moment when the world will realize the truth about this unappreciated and misunderstood servant:

Behold, my servant shall prosper, he shall be exalted and lifted up, and shall be very high. As many were astonished at him—his appearance was so marred, beyond human semblance, and his form beyond that of the sons of men—so shall he startle many nations; kings shall shut their mouths because of him; for that which has not been told them they shall see, and that which they have not heard they shall understand. (Isa. 52:13-15)

And Israel, in anticipation of such glory, ceased to be afraid. She said to God: "Nevertheless I am continually with thee, . . . My flesh and my heart may fail, but God is the strength of my heart and my portion for ever" (Ps. 73:23-26). And the Eternal answered: "For a brief moment I forsook you, but with great compassion I will gather you" (Isa 54·7) "I have loved you with an everlasting love; therefore I have continued my faithfulness to you" (Jer. 31:3)

We began by examining that question about God's name, that is, the question about God's reality. It is a question that expresses man's entire need and perplexity vis-à-vis God and at the same time his importunity and zeal to use God. And we spoke about God's answer: "I will be present as I will be present." We are now in a better position to comprehend what this statement says about God's faithfulness and at the same time about his untouchable freedom to be present as he wills. There is in the patriarchal history a brief scene that shows that very faithfulness and freedom of God in an incomparable way (see Gen. 48). The aged, blind Jacob desires before he dies to bless Joseph's sons. Joseph has brought the boys to the bed in such a way that Jacob's right hand will rest upon the head of Joseph's first-born son, Manasseh, and his left hand upon the head of Joseph's second-born son, Ephraim. But Jacob sits up, crosses his arms, and lays his right hand upon Ephraim's head. Joseph intervenes; he thinks his father has made a mistake: "Not so, my father; for this one is the first-born!" But Jacob persists: "I know, my son, I know." What was it the blind man might have known? "I will be present as I will be present!"

As I conclude, I want to speak briefly once more about what I did not intend in this address. I hope you have not expected, now that the problems in individual matters have been formulated and discussed, that the theologian would propound the answer and solve the problem. We evangelicals do not know such a function of theology. What I said to you was a contribution that has to be considered along with the contributions you yourselves have to make. But since theology too is a science in which honest work is accomplished, and since it is concerned more than other scholarly disciplines with ultimate, human questions, it too must be heard in the general discussion. For it believes that it occupies a kind of guardian position in the circle of human knowledge, as was said, for example, to the prophet Ezekiel: "Son of man, I have made you a watchman for the house of Israel" (3:17). This position of watchman consists in the obligation to warn. In the sense, therefore, of that which has concerned us in this lecture, theology has to warn man against the unending danger of myth, which in the form of scientific myth waits to take us captive; theology must warn against all absolutes that produce short circuits. Indeed, it must do so even in cases of scientific constructs like "nature" or "history," i.e., of harmless formulas that require us to construe them with discernment, but which must always be either altered or replaced by better ones! It ought to be the task of theology to sharpen the senses so that one will recognize the much greater danger that attends such absolutes: subjectively, to be sure, a more honest, but also a profoundly more terrible zeal to erect images about oneself that make it at times impossible for one to attend to God's revelation, God who is indeed much more hidden and revealed than any deep mythicizing knows. I spoke about nature and history because I could mention only a few examples. I could also have mentioned what we mean when we say man. Our choice of words—and it is more than a matter of inept usage—is so benumbed in this regard that it requires effort for us to realize that what we are accustomed to call man does not exist, that to speak of man is not only to use an inadequate abstraction, but a most dangerous one that belongs to that iconostasis we were talking about. I am thinking about that idea of man which makes all thinking and questioning have to begin with him, and from whose standpoint then a possible relationship of man to God, among other things, would be a subject for reflection. The Bible says that is putting the cart before the horse, for it does not know man who can debate the question of his relationship to God. Rather, it says in the statement about his being created in God's image that man is understood only when one begins with God. Everything about him points to the upper world of God. Indeed, he has his origin—that's what it says—in the depths of the divine heart: "Then God said, 'Let us make man in our image, after our likeness' " (Gen. 1:26).

But theology ought not simply to proclaim this warning against myth from the window or the rooftops. It ought also to heed it earnestly in its own house. Theology would be very naive if it were to think that only the heathen were subject to such danger, for a Christian is constantly in danger of believing in myths and serving idols. There is, indeed, not a single statement of his faith that he could not misuse in an idolatrous manner. And theology must certainly lead the way in that flexibility and inner freedom that shatters favorite statements, for it is true that nontheologians are dogmatically much more strongly tied to tradition. That does not mean, of course, that Christian faith should become unconditionally conformed to the world. The troubling question, whether and in what domains it should do so, whether it should go out courageously to "beat the bushes," or in obedience to another biblical text, "enter its chambers and shut the doors behind it until the wrath is past" (Isa. 26:20)—that is ultimately a question of the charisma God grants to his church, and therefore a question about its future which we do not have to decide.

But no one should think that this function of giving warning is a gloomy one that can be exercised only in resignation. On the contrary, it is a function of joy. Theology knows, or should ever be aware, that man lives in a world in which day speaks to day and night to night about the incomprehensible glory of the Creator; and it knows, or should know, that in what we call history God is preparing this world for his kingdom, and that what we call time is going to meet that which no eye has seen and no ear heard. And on the way there? Now if we succeed in getting rid of the images and idols, we will know that we are hidden in God's hands. Eliphaz once said to his rebelling friend, Job, If you were right with God, then you would also find yourself right with everything that now disturbs you. "You shall be in league with the stones of the field that dull your plow, and the beasts of the field (that eat your crops) shall be at peace with you" (Job 5:23).

But to see things in this way, to know that one's life is in God's hands, is certainly not a method for knowing the world that we could demonstrate; it is not a general trust and not an available key that we could mass produce and hand out. It is something quite different. It is a mission. To believe in the reality of God is a gift of the Holy Ghost.

"A sower went out to sow. And as he sowed, some seed fell along the path, and the birds came and devoured it. Other seed fell on rocky ground, where it had not much soil, and immediately it sprang up, since it had no depth of soil; and when the sun rose it was scorched, and since it had no root it withered away. Other seed fell among thorns and the thorns grew up and choked it, and it yielded no grain. And other seeds fell into good soil and brought forth grain, growing up and increasing and yielding thirtyfold and sixtyfold and a hundredfold." And he said, "He who has ears to hear, let him hear." (Mark 4:3-9)

13

THE ORIGIN
OF MOSAIC MONOTHEISM

(Lecture on radio RIAS, Berlin, November 1961. The title of the lecture was assigned by the station's editorial staff.)

With respect to an assessment of monotheism, matters seem to be quite clear for many people today: every child knows that monotheism is good and proper while polytheism is wrong; and if the origin of monotheism is mentioned, then many may well suppose that it can concern only the arduous, perhaps, but not blockable road to reconstructing a perception that today, at least in our own culture, is established for every believer. Who would want to say of himself that he is a polytheist?

This conception of monotheism as a more or less general human stage of knowledge reached by Judaism, secured and propagated by Christianity, from which one can no longer politely retreat, first arose in the period of the Enlightenment and haunts many heads today. The curious views that the Frenchman Ernest Renan expressed did not prevail because the scientific foundation on which they rested was too flimsy. In Renan's view Israel's religion was monotheistic from the beginning, but that monotheism is not to be valued very highly; it is to be explained as arising from a lack of religious imagination, from the metaphysical sterility and meager religious requirements of the Semites. Thus Renan condemns Israel's monotheism for what, as we will see, is its most important particularity: that it is not the fruit of an abstract, rational discussion with polytheism.

Now such discussion is a well-known phenomenon to the student of religion, for in polytheistic religions a need arises now and then, after a unification of frequently proliferating conceptions, to reach a uniform view. But first one must doubt whether discussions of that sort ever lead to consistent, monotheistic religion (it is therefore better to talk about monotheistic tendencies), and second one must doubt that Mosaic monotheism originated from such speculative reduction or from the need for a uniform view; in fact one can be certain that it did not. It will be the task of this lecture to show that what one can still call Mosaic monotheism is something quite different from and, I may say, something much more foreign to the popular religious thought of today. Do not be disappointed, therefore, ladies and gentlemen, if the answer I have to give is not quite so simple as to be carried home with confidence, it could be, indeed, that to pose the alternative monotheism, polytheism postulates a system of thought into which the phenomenon of Mosaic faith cannot be incorporated at all.

Let us begin with a concrete example. David is being pursued by Saul, and in the Judaean hill country the two opponents find themselves on opposite sides of a ravine, engaged in a remarkable dialogue. Only one sentence of it interests us here. David asks why he is being pursued; are there perhaps in the background those who would drive him out from "the heritage of the Lord, saying, 'Go, serve other gods.' Now therefore, let not my blood fall to the earth away from the presence of the Lord" (I Sam. 26:19-20). David sees the most extreme possibility approaching, that he will have to depart from the land; and as a man of antiquity he knows that exile from the circle of the national union will have for him an extreme consequence: he will have to serve other gods. One can scarcely say that the narrator of this story considered David to be a monotheist. But a polytheist? No one who knows his way among ancient texts will feel comfortable with that assertion, for the meaning of David's statement was that the superior power of external circumstances could prevent him from exclusive worship of Israel's God. What more can one say? Indeed, if Israel had had anything like a doctrine of God that was normative for all time and that we could consult, we would have our answer easily. But Israel had no such dogmatic system.

She had something else: a command of God that forbade her to worship all other gods. "I am the Lord your God, you shall have no other gods before me." That is the first commandment of the decalogue that in substance at least goes back most probably to the Mosaic period, i.e., long before the Palestinian period of Israel's history. Clearly it reckons with cults surrounding other gods; and the fact that Israel's God has a proper name points, as has been rightly said, to a basically polytheistic situation. But there is also that other element, that abrupt claim to exclusiveness, which forbade Israel to serve any other god in any other form. This passionate claim to exclusiveness is, in such a radical form, something unique in the history of religions, for the cults of the gods in antiquity were very tolerant. They demanded but one thing, namely, that they be recognized for their own sacred value. But Israel would not grant this recognition, and that was from the beginning the ground for conflict in her relationship to the cults of other gods.

If we inquire further into the circumstances of this actually mysterious phenomenon, we encounter the conception, so characteristic for Israel's faith, of God's zeal. The prophet Hosea ventured to say that God is as jealous as a lover to be the only one. It is interesting to see that the statement about God's zeal appears wherever exclusive worship of the God of Israel is mentioned. Israel's God does not mean to share with other powers his claim to reverence and trust. When Israel decided on that day of assembly at Shechem, perhaps a bit too confidently, to cleave to this God alone, she heard Joshua say, "You cannot serve the Lord; for he is a holy God; he is a jealous God" (Josh. 24:19).

Here we see already that the exclusive claim of the first

commandment was something incomparably more demanding than what we understand by monotheism, because it presses its demand for a decision much more firmly on a man's conscience. And that provided matter for conflict in ancient Israel's faith in God. For even if this weighty first commandment long remained only a matter of interest inside Israel alone, and even though Israel may have recognized the gods of the nations as realities and powers, still that recognition was from the start strangely broken and relative. For the *way* in which Israel understood God's revelation was profoundly different from that of the religions of neighboring peoples. They served their gods with images. Israel worshiped God without representations. The prohibition to worship God in any representation is not, as has often been thought, an effusion of Israel's more spiritual conception of God. The philosophical contrast between material and spiritual is not involved here, and besides there are cultic representations that reveal a highly spiritual conception of deity. The problem was not that idolatry was not spiritual enough, but rather *what* the representation actually revealed.

Religions that worship God in images have the following beliefs. Everywhere in this world of ours divine mysteries break open in which the divine reveals itself. The world would be a dark room; but now, if I may say it this way, windows have been pushed open everywhere from the world of the gods, and through them the divine shines in and man can partake of the blessing of divine powers. He can participate in the earth's fertility and the order of the stars; indeed at every place in the world there exists at least the possibility that it will be transparent for the divine and empowered to be a symbol and statement from God. And to that Israel said no. Not because that form of worship called in question the wonder of creation; it said incomparable things about it. But there is at work in these cults with their images and thoughtful symbols nothing more than a conversation of created things with one another. Israel was convinced that God is both much more hidden from and at the same time much nearer to man.

This knowledge about the profound delusion of all idolatry, this refusal to recognize all the enticing voices from the depths of creation as a revelation of God himself, these were only the result, the consequence of something different that had gone before. Israel found herself addressed by God from the beginning. She knew herself to be seized bý him and drawn into a conversation. But in all that, it must be said, Israel had not become religiously transfigured. Rather, she uttered a witness against herself, a testimony of her fright and ever-renewed despair before this divine address. But then she began with time to realize that she knew God, not from the symbolic language of cultic images, but from his word that went forth always new, and that she lived from this word alone. Life—how relatively constant is the idea in religions that life is an innerworldly, sacred power and that men can succeed by some rite or myth in freeing a passage to this mystery! And how cool and clear is the statement laid in the mouth of Moses in Deuteronomy: "Man does not live by bread alone, but . . . by everything that proceeds out of the mouth of the Lord" (8:3)

I was speaking earlier of the controversial material that is associated with the beginning of ancient Israel's faith in God. Now we see that it was part of the particularity of God's revelation that had been granted to this people. Israel knew she was bound to that divine word made manifest in history—how often does the Old Testament say that the word of the Lord came to XY—and not to the timeless, symbolic language of cultic images. One could imagine, therefore, that it was a short distance to an actual denial of the gods of other peoples. But the matter was not quite so simple.

Israel entered Canaan as a nomadic people that had roamed with its sheep and goats through the steppe between places of water and pasture, but later she became sedentary. The meaning of this adaptation is difficult for us in the West to appreciate, since our lives are not bound to a definite cultural region with its specific and limited conditions of life. The religion of these erstwhile nomads and shepherds had to adjust to the completely new circumstances of their lives. Ancient Israel now saw herself confronted by a fact that she had previously not seriously included in her religious value system: the fecund earth. The fecund earth in antiquity was not some natural phenomenon like the sea or mountains or desert. Rather it harbored a divine mystery, and therefore a man could not simply till it; he required divine warrant and guidance in order to avail himself of its blessing. In Canaan there existed the worship of a divinity who could provide that; the god was Baal, god of weather and fecundity, who was worshiped at just those sanctuaries to which Israel, who had now become an agricultural people, felt herself directed.

That suggests the great crisis that occurred in Israel's religion after she entered Canaan. Was the God of Sinai, the God of the ten commandments and election, also the giver of the blessing of the fertile soil? Was it not rather Baal? How then was the relation of Israel's God to the whole Canaanite pantheon to be defined? Even more, was Israel's God the creator of the world and—the horizon continually expanded—was he also the lord of history?

The answer to all these enormous questions could not come from a sudden act of thinking or from a simple religious process of reasoning. No, it had to be experienced as a reality out of Israel's faith, as a fact that Yahweh, not Baal, was lord of the earth. That required the religious vigilance of generations. The retrospective telling of Israel's history did not gloss over the fact that it contained much error, much defection from the faith of the fathers and above all much unwholesome confusion of Yahweh and Baal. But the fact that Israel's faith withstood this crisis, that it was capable of understanding Israel's God as also the giver of fertility, indeed the creator of the world and the lord of history, that fact also decided, paradoxically, the question of monotheism. It is paradoxical because Israel, in the time after this crisis, did not deny any power to the strange gods.

I mentioned a moment ago the pantheon that Israel

discovered to exist in Canaan. There is in the Psalter a strange poem that describes a very dramatic occurrence. Israel's God appears in this pantheon, i.e., in the assembly of Canaanite gods, to reproach them severely for showing themselves incapable of maintaining justice and order among their peoples. "How long will you judge unjustly and show partiality to the wicked? . . . I thought you were gods . . . but you shall die like men" (Ps. 82). I do not think that this talk of the gods is merely rhetorical. The poem derives from a genuine struggle with the unsolved problem of strange gods. On the other hand, the psalm asserts the superiority of Israel's God, who is completely capable of ordering these gods to appear before his seat of judgment. The way out, the solution, which appears at the end of the poem, is magnificent, indeed prophetic: This failure, the powerlessness of those who should be the guarantors of justice and order, can end only in a final and conclusive removal of power from these gods.

But up to the time about which I will speak in a moment, there were only occasional expressions like that about the gods of the peoples. There were, of course, some occasions, as, e.g., in times of war when Israel was in enemy territory, when Israel did address the question of other gods. How that was done depended on the outlook of the narrator in question. When, for example, the Israelite army, in the days of the prophet Elisha, besieged the Moabite capital, that king in his despair sacrificed his own son on the city wall (II Kings 3). That brought the anger of Chemosh, god of the Moabites, upon Israel, as the narrator says, so that the Israelites had to give up the siege. Certainly, such a realistic conception of the power of a foreign god is rather isolated in the Old Testament, but that does not mean that this narrator had inadequate notions about Israel's God.

Ancient Israel had much in her own house to set in order, for she knew that she had to obey the first commandment; and that, as we have already seen, caused her great problems. Every generation had to take a responsible stand on the question, what does it mean, here and now, to serve only Yahweh, the God of Israel, to obey him and to trust him? What does it mean in view of the widely practiced cult of the dead? Were the spirits of the dead such powers that it was prudent to offer sacrifices to the dead? We see how the earlier sacred law of Israel was applied against even the most harmless form of the cult of the dead. Here, in a daily religious guerrilla war, Israel made those great decisions; for the question of the first commandment, whether Israel is ready to entrust herself to her God alone, was not answered by the emergence of a consistently monotheistic outlook.

There was another question. What about serious illnesses? Were there demonic powers of the underworld at work in them, powers one could withstand only by performing sacred rites? Israel thought otherwise. The narrator who tells of Saul's melancholy and gloom expresses the matter this way: "Now the Spirit of the Lord departed from Saul, and an evil spirit from the Lord tormented him" (I Sam. 16:14). This statement is unique in the history of religion, for religions take pains to separate what is dark and destructive from the gods and to derive those forces from the realm of the lower malign powers. The calm certainty with which Israel accepted what is dark and incomprehensible from God's hand, the way she resisted the obvious temptation to escape into philosophical dualism, was something incomparably more important than the question of whether she reckoned with the power of gods outside the realm of her own cultic worship or even considered those gods to have no power.

To be sure, however, there came a time when the question about the might of the gods of the nations became urgent. That was when the Assyrian kings sent their armies into Palestine and began to gather up the small Syrian states. That made the question, who then was lord in the realm of history, unavoidable; and the times had passed when Israel was free to answer the question about the competence of the gods one way or another. Was this world power that set about stretching its hand toward Jerusalem stronger than Israel's God, and had God perhaps not taken account of it at all in his plans for history?

Isaiah doubtless gave his two contemporaries an extremely perplexing answer to that. "In that day the Lord will whistle for the fly which is at the sources of the streams of Egypt, and for the bee which is in the land of Assyria. . . . In that day the Lord will shave with a razor which is hired beyond the River. . . . the head and the hair of the feet, and it will sweep away the beard also." The prophet's vision is monstrous: just as a shepherd guides his flock by whistling or snapping his fingers, so God directs world empires. He is the one who summons the Assyrians to Palestine. The Assyrian empire looming on the horizon did not obstruct the prophets' view of God. On the contrary, the proportions are backwards. The Assyrian empire has no independent power at all, and there is nothing in the prophetic vision about Assyrian gods. Assyria is a razor, a tool that God uses once to effect his plans. Not the empire but only God's plans fill the historical realm.

In this view of history the gods of other peoples have no room at all; they are deprived of power. No wonder that Isaiah, in the wonderful poem in which he sees God's self-realization in history approaching, can speak only with grim humor about the fate of idols and idol worshipers. "In that day men will cast forth their idols of silver and their idols of gold, which they made for themselves to worship, to the moles and to the bats, to enter the caverns of the rocks and the clefts of the cliffs, from before the terror of the Lord, and from the glory of his majesty" (Isa. 2:20-21). Here is monotheism indeed, even though it is not intentional. But it is much more than monotheism; in Isaiah we meet an ultimate comforting message that interprets man's existence in history with reference to God's coming and therewith the removal of power from the idols.

The prophet who expresses most clearly what we understand as monotheism is second Isaiah, who lived nearly two centuries after Isaiah. Again, his concern is with the interpretation of a world experience of supreme importance, the appearance of the Persian Cyrus and therewith the transfer of world power to the Indo-Europeans. And now God speaks to this Cyrus, "I am the Lord, and there is no other, besides me there is no God; I gird you, though you do not know me, that men may know, from the rising of the sun and from the west, that there is none besides me; I am the Lord, and there is no other" (Isa. 45:5-6). The universally-oriented view of this prophet is incomparable; nevertheless, one must keep in mind that this prophet espouses a decided historical particularism: Israel and what God reveals through her is the center of world history. That is the point to which the prophet directs the attention of all the peoples: "Turn to me and be saved, all the ends of the earth! For I am God, and there is no other" (Isa. 45:22).

One must keep in mind that the one who spoke that way was the member of a small, politically destroyed people, whose influential leaders, deported as they were, found themselves in a hopeless situation. And just in this circumstance, in which many an Israelite may have asked himself whether the gods of the Babylonians had not shown themselves stronger, in this moment arose the prophet who was persuaded as no other of the world significance of Israel's God. Under the pressure of one of the most severe troubles, it was given to Israel's faith to entertain this ultimate experience of the world significance of her God. Let no one think that was an experience achieved by way of religious or philosophical arguments. Rather, it came through the endurance of severe troubles and the confirmation, indeed a completely new certainty, into which faith in this time was led.

Let me cite a text in that connection that is also characteristic for our question about monotheism. It contains what is almost a vision of a world judgment, to which Israel's God invites the gods of the peoples. It is now to be clearly understood who has called the Persian Cyrus to the political stage of the world: the gods or the God of Israel? The nations are assembled, for now everything depends on the evidence to be given by the witnesses. "You are my witnesses," says the Lord . . .

"that you may know and believe me. . . . Before me no god was formed, nor shall there be any after me. I, I am the Lord, and besides me there is no savior" (Isa. 43:10-11).

Let it be said once more: Here monotheism is expressed with all the clarity one could desire. But is it not remarkable that there is talk of the idols who are invited to the trial? Is that only rhetorical makeup? To think so is to misunderstand the prophet. He does not speak of a general philosophical truth but makes a confession. But in the view of this confession lies the other possibility which faith has rejected. Monotheism is a thesis the truth of which a philosopher could possibly unfold. But the prophet believes that the singleness of God as the Lord of world history and as the only helper can be made believable only by those who bear witness to him; and he leaves no doubt that those who bear witness to him will have to assert themselves against an oppressive majority. Monotheism could be a truth, which, once perceived, is settled for all time. The confession to God that says, "besides Thee there is no savior," this confession of great trust is never settled forever, but must be ventured again and again.

14

GOD'S WORD
IN HISTORY ACCORDING
TO THE OLD TESTAMENT

(Manuscript of a lecture from 1941. Later additions have, where possible, been included in this version.)

We begin with a thesis, which is the presupposition to all that follows: "History is God's proceeding" (L. Köhler); and we add to that, *real* history, not a line which a people draws from myth to itself in time. Such a line is disguised myth. When we read in old Babylonian tradition that in the beginning kingship descended from heaven to the southern Babylonian city Eridu, and when we see that the Babylonian story of creation concludes with the founding of the city of Babylon by the god, we know we are dealing with a myth in which historical Babylon celebrates its ultimate, divine origin. Modern, more secular forms of this mythical way of thinking are familiar to us. But observe how completely differently the Old Testament community thinks of itself in history. This line does not run directly from the creation of the world to saving history, but rather to the plainly universal aspect of the table of nations in which all the nations are presented equally as creation of God (Gen. 10). The theological significance of that chapter lies in its emphasis on this universal; and just in her putting aside all thoughts about God's saving activity Israel was not afraid to see herself quite unmythically within the world of nations. To see herself? Indeed, where then is Israel in the table of nations? Abraham, the ancestor of Israel, is not named in it. Imagine, Israel is represented in the table of nations by a name that is completely neutral for the later history of faith, by the name of Arpachshad, who is in addition the ancestor of many other, mostly anonymous tribes and groups. That means that Israel took her existence in history very seriously indeed. Any flight into myth was impossible, for behind Israel lay the sea of nations from which she had come. That which Israel experienced of God was thus actual historical revelation.

Seven genealogical members succeed Arpachshad, and only then do we touch upon Abraham. Here in Genesis 12 the universal aspect is suddenly narrowed to the particular. God's history with the world, which was one of increasing alienation, breaks off; and saving history begins.

I have to justify this theological term, saving history. To do that, we must make a small detour. In Deuteronomy 26:5-10 we find a formulary statement that was to be spoken when the first fruits of the field were presented to God:

> "A wandering Aramean was my father; and he went down into Egypt and sojourned there, few in number; and there he became a nation, great, mighty, and populous. And the Egyptians treated us harshly, and afflicted us, and laid upon us hard bondage. Then we cried to the Lord the God of our fathers, and the Lord heard our voice, and saw our affliction, our toil, and our oppression; and the Lord brought us out of Egypt with a mighty hand and an outstretched arm, with great terror, with signs and wonders; and he brought us into this place and gave us this land, a land flowing with milk and honey. And behold, now I bring the first of the fruit of the ground, which thou, O Lord, hast given me."

The presentation of the first fruits of the ground was a cultic observance, as a part of which the worshiper had to offer a kind of prayer that was assuredly old and traditional. But it was not a real prayer. The Deuteronomic text speaks of God in the third person, and only in the final statement is there a personal address to God. What the worshiper does is to recapitulate the chief events of saving history: the age of the patriarchs, entrance into Egypt, oppression, liberation, and conquest of the land. He does not pray, but he confesses God's acts of salvation in history; he speaks a credo, and it is interesting to see that already in the most ancient cult of ancient Israel there was a place at which God's saving acts that had constituted the community were recited as a confession. There are many such shorter or longer recapitulations in the Old Testament of the saving acts that brought Israel into being, and they all derive in principle and in form from that ancient cultic credo.

We now take a giant leap, leaving out all possible connecting links, and ask about the Hexateuch, the books Genesis to Joshua. What was the actual purpose of this gigantic work that stretches from primeval history, through the patriarchs to the conquest of Canaan? Every one of the source-documents of the Hexateuch has this same outline; each of them, except for the prehistoric introduction, runs from the patriarchal era to the conquest of Canaan. That is, they all follow that canonical scheme of saving history that already existed in the ancient credo; for the entire Hexateuch is nothing else than a credo that has been enormously developed and incredibly enriched with all possibly retrievable sacred traditions. It is a confession of saving history, embellished like baroque and permeated theologically to the last detail. We have, then, a rather grotesque phenomenon. Imagine, God has accompanied a few men—in the end several tribes—on a journey through history. The journey is not very long, and in the judgment of world history it is completely without consequence. But because the journey was with the living God, the descendants of those original travelers have brought together tradition after tradition and created a work that is pushed to the very limits of readability—all for the sake of recording this rather short journey of God's with all its events. I think that is a fact that should be considered from all points of view. But now we come to our special theme: what, here and elsewhere in the Old Testament, is God's relationship to the history of this community and this people?

It seems an easy question to answer, for at the beginning of the sacred story is the command to Abraham: "Go from your country and your kindred and your father's house to the land that I will show you" (Gen. 12:1). The answer to the question, then, is clearly this: that a word from God set this history in motion. We will have to concern ourselves with that in a moment, but first, this event has fallen a little too neatly into our lap, so to speak; and that does not permit us to suspect, if we do that sort of thing, the theological background of this testimony. We must therefore consider the matter a bit more in detail, for in the Hexateuch there are so many traditions, brought together from so many theological perspectives, that this statement of God to Abraham is rather like the signature before a musical staff.

In the Old Testament—we now extend our study to the entire Old Testament—we find witness to three kinds of divine historical acts. I will outline them briefly; theology has to be able to distinguish them at all times.

First, God acts in history in miracles. The miracle of the Red Sea (Exod. 14) is paradigmatic. There the emphasis lies less on the miraculous physical phenomenon than on God's enigmatic attack on the Egyptian army. The wheels of their chariots are retarded by a mysterious power; the Egyptian infantry column does not come near the Israelites because of the intervening cloud which causes confusion in the hostile army. It turns out that all activity proceeds exclusively from God; the Israelites are in no way active in their own defense. *God* will get the glory, as Exod. 14:17 says explicity. We ought to spend much more time with this expression. It is frequent in the Old Testament, and it always marks those passages where the otherwise hidden glory of the divine activity appears in history superficially, so to speak, recognizable to the eye of faith.

Take a picturesque example: Gideon's victory over the Midianites (Judg. 7). In the history of literature that is a heroic legend; but to call it that is misleading, for at the climactic moment in the story Gideon is anything but a "hero." God's test of the men at the water to reduce the size of the army already introduces the actual state of affairs: God requires no great levy of troops, indeed he does not require even this small one, for they stand around the camp, swing their torches, break their pots, blow their trumpets, and remain standing as though rooted; not one draws his sword. Rather, as the Old Testament says it, the fear of God fell upon the enemy, a panic in which they acted in complete confusion and killed each other. This story makes even clearer that where God gets the glory no cooperative action by men exists. Gideon and his men perform grotesque gestures, but God is the sole actor. One cannot say, of course, that the story lets everything human fade into a shadow for the sake of the divine act. On the contrary, it is extremely graphic in all details; but at the climax of the action, the hero's part is unexpectedly taken from his hands, and the miracle settles into a hollow that is completely free of all human initiative (similarly II Chron. 20). This is the oldest form of testimony in the history of Old Testament faith about God's activity in history, but it is not separated from other representations. Rather it retains its place in the chorus of the ancient witnesses, as Daniel 3 shows, down to the latest periods of Israel's history.

The second kind of representation of divine action in history is quite different, indeed really opposed to what has just been sketched. The story of Joseph serves as a good example. But where does it speak in clarification and elucidation about God? Only at the end, after it has led the reader through a tangle of conflicts, through all heights and depths, does it open up its profound mystery in the words of Joseph (Gen. 50:20): "You meant evil against me; but God meant it for good." What had the story shown up to that point? In one long chapter after another it has shown *men*, as they treat each other, reveal the abysmal depths of their hearts, and thereby cause each other to suffer. Only at the very end, when God has resolved everything for good, does one learn that God has held the reins in his hand all along and has directed everything, even where no one could have assumed it any longer. But how? No miracle ever occurred. Rather, God's leading has worked in secret, in the plans and thoughts of men's hearts, who have savagely gone about *their own* business. Thus the field for the divine providence is the human heart. One would ask in vain how God intervened here. The immanently causal connection of the events was as tight as possible; there was no gap, no hollow spot set aside for God's intervention. God did his work in the decisions of men. I dare to assert that the story brushes the risky thought that God was at work in man's sin, a consequence of the divine omnipotence that the Old Testament otherwise carefully avoids.

Now that is quite a different witness to God's action in history. God's work is completely hidden in the secular, but understood much more fully. It is included not only intermittently in miracles (particularly those of the holy war), but continually and equally in all areas of life, sacred as well as profane. This kind of representation occurs in those texts that move so fully in the realm of the profane that one could almost think they were actually concerned with quite profane history. Consider, for example, the detailed story of Absalom's conspiracy (II Sam. 15 ff.) and the end of David's reign or the story of the fall of the Davidic-Solomonic empire (I Kings 12). Still, the attentive reader will find even there that uplifted finger that points, as in the story of Joseph, to the effective and all-directing power above the historical stage. Consider the statement in I Kings 12:15, after Rehoboam has followed the counsel of his young advisers, "it was a turn of affairs brought about by the Lord" (cf. also II Sam. 17:14; Judg. 9:23). These references are almost always quite brief, almost shy; and then the narrator again draws the curtain together before the end, and everything continues its former course, apparently in normal, causal sequence. That, then, is the second kind of representation; we may call it the "profane historical activity." It is so clear that this very short suggestion is perhaps sufficient. In its period this cool, realistic view of history is intimately connected with the Solomonic enlightenment, in which the ancient, archaic conceptions of the previous era underwent a profound transformation.

The third kind of representation is again different, and here it is difficult to remain brief. We shall have a look at the writing of history that we have particularly in the two books of Kings, which we call Deuteronomistic. That writing, as we have it today, can be understood only against the background of a major fact, the catastrophe of 586 B.C. and the Exile. In the eyes of those men who speak to us in this historical writing, the destruction of their national existence was the least significant aspect of the catastrophe. The situation became frightful and full of despair when *God* spoke a categorical and apparently final no. *God's* history suddenly stood still for these men, and in this frightful situation, without any saving history, the penetrating question arose: How could all that happen? How could God, from whom one had the most certain promises, nevertheless reject his people? That is the question. And now they leafed through past history, examining page after page, and reached the elementary conclusion that God was not at fault. On the contrary, God had manifested unequalled long-suffering. But the nation had heaped one faithless deed upon another; it had disobeyed the commandments and gone after the gods of Nature, and so God, after long waiting had to lead his people into judgment. It is a historical account of expiation that this theological school composed in the Exile. (Whether this situation of being in exile without a history was a suitable presupposition for the rise of history-writing, can be doubted. Many shortcomings of this work are indeed traceable to the fact that its authors had no immediate relationship to actual historical events any more.) But now to our real question: How is God's action in history seen theologically here? This school did not, of course, write history anew, from the beginning. It assembled all the documents and pieces that had been earlier written down and worked them into a great composition. Their own part they expressed only in the framework and in some theological insertions. Thus the theological line of the whole is not uniform and not everything included in the work has been consistently edited theologically. On the other hand, the theological scheme imposed on the historical work is easy to recognize literarily, and so we have the theological conception that is intended to be decisive for understanding the whole work.

We will understand these historians only when we realize that for them three things were given: 1) the actual course of events ending in the catastrophe of the northern kingdom in 722 and the southern kingdom in 586 B.C.; 2) the revealed will of God, especially in the book of Deuteronomy; and 3) the promise to David's house (Nathan's prophecy, II Sam. 7). And now the work proceeds in such a way that it judges and interprets the first thing, the actual course of history, by the last-named facts, the commandments and the promise to David. "In the twenty-third year of Joash, . . . Jehoahaz the son of Jehu began to reign over Israel in Samaria, and he . . . did what was evil in the sight of the Lord, . . . and the anger of the Lord was kindled against Israel, and he gave them continually into the hand of Hazael king of Syria" (II Kings 13:1-3). Thus in almost every chapter, and then as the northern kingdom finally collapsed under the blows of the Assyrians, the historian finds words for a melancholy epilogue: "And this was so, because the people of Israel had sinned against the Lord their God. . . . And the Lord rejected all the descendants of Israel . . . and gave them into the hand of spoilers, until he had cast them out of his sight" (II Kings 17:7-20).

In this we see clearly that God's word is the key to the history of salvation. God has given his commandments, and he has threatened severe judgments as the consequence of disobedience. Those judgments have occurred. In this respect, therefore, everything is quite clear (almost *too* clear, as we will see below): God has exercised long and renewed patience (God's long-suffering is a most

important thought in this writing of history!), but in the
end, when the frightful sins of Manasseh were added to
all the rest, God let the great judgment irrupt. What is
one to think of this long, effective patience of God, his
enduring and forgiving acts over centuries of history?
Was it just God's friendly attitude, about which there is
nothing more to say except that God has it at times? No!
This enduring and forgiving activity of God is to be
explained as his loyalty to his promise to David. That
promise was the actual restraining and guarding power in
those centuries when the sins and faithless deeds of the
people should have brought down manifold judgment.
Examples of this less familiar basic idea can be seen in
I Kings: Solomon is told of the dissolution of his empire as
the judgment for his sins, "However I will not tear away all
the kingdom . . . for the sake of David my servant" (11:13)
"that David my servant may always have a lamp before
me" (v. 36). In I Kings 15:3 we read about Abijam that "he
walked in all the sins which his father did before him," but
"for David's sake the Lord his God gave him a lamp in
Jerusalem." Also Joram, Jehoshaphat's son, did what
displeased God, "yet the Lord would not destroy Judah, for
the sake of David his servant, since he promised to give a
lamp to him and to his sons for ever" (II Kings 8:19). Here
one sees especially clearly the way history is understood in
this work: the actual organizing power behind all
historical events is God's word, which works itself out
creatively in history both in judgment and in protecting
well being. We will pursue this strange theologoumenon
still further, but here we ask, In the end did God's anger
triumph over his saving promise? The conclusion to the
great work is strange enough. It reports extensively on
God's great punitive judgment on Jerusalem. But at the
very end there is a most curious note. After a thirty year
term in prison, King Jehoiachin was released, not freed,
but called in honor to dine regularly at the table of the king
of Babylon. At the outermost limit of the historical work,
therefore, there is something like a faint clearing in the
darkness of God's judgment. The historian was *unable* to

147

believe that God's saving work for David's house had really been completely abandoned. As little as he knew he had no warrant to take less than dead seriously the horror of the judgment, still his faith suspected that that judgment was perhaps not God's very last word. In any case, he mentioned that event with which, if he so willed, God could again begin in grace.

We can further support our statement about the power of God's word in history by referring to those passages in which a historical event is mentioned that was previously foretold by a prophet and now brought to pass by God in order to establish the prophetic word (II Kings 14:25). Here too is the idea that God's word is what really makes history, as we saw earlier with respect to God's word to Abraham that first set the whole story of salvation in motion. We will discuss this fact better, however, in the context of the actual prophetic witnesses in the Old Testament. The difference between the Deuteronomistic view of history and that of the prophets is generally that the former sees the goals of God's historical activity as immanent in history, while the prophets speak of God's bringing history to a consummation. A critique of such a historical view is, of course, indispensable. What is at issue is a theological system that can be forced on history only with violence. The authors were not infrequently forced to correct history. We also have to recognize in the Deuteronomistic system a formula, which by means of a law seeks to master the divine activity and therein occasionally infringes its freedom and mystery. That, however, will not confuse the one who knows that in every human witness there is both revelation and human obfuscation.

But now to the prophets. Here it is almost indispensable that we consider first the prophets' own relationship to the Word. That relationship is quite exceptional and much more direct than elsewhere among men who hear the word. Jeremiah says that he ate the words of God as they came to him (15:16). We will do well not to consider that as an exaggerated, metaphorical statement. It is a relationship of spontaneity, indeed of vital concern for the Word. The prophets know more than the normally faithful do about man's being dependent on God's word. I think about the statement regarding hunger for God's word, a statement in Amos 8:11 f. that evokes an unlimited weakened condition that even extends to the physical. And from Ezekiel we hear that he received his message in the form of a scroll that he was to eat and that its frightful word of judgment tasted sweet as honey to him (3:1-3). To such an extent had he given up all human sensibilities; to such an extent had God come to him and made him *his* mouth! We spoke of the power of the Word according to the understanding of the prophets. It is always the same. For the prophets the word of God is a distinct reality that encounters them almost as something material. They therefore see the relationship of this word to history as also something almost material, in any case as an indescribably effective power. What was said to us rather rigidly and without color in the Deuteronomic history we now hear in the overpowering exposition of prophetic speech: "The Lord has sent a word against Jacob, and it will light upon Israel" (Isa. 9:8). The prophet sees a word break in like a meteor and unleash a series of punitive judgments. Nothing at all is said about a content of which men are spiritually to take cognizance.

Jeremiah was called to prophesy against peoples and kingdoms, to root up and to destroy, to build up and to plant. By what means? How can that be expected of Jeremiah? He will accomplish it by virtue of the word that he enters into history. That is the way the oft-quoted statement of Jeremiah 23:29 is to be understood: God's word is "like a hammer which breaks the rock in pieces"; its dynamic force breaks all resistance. Second Isaiah sharply distinguishes this creative word as the only thing to endure among all other historical facts: "Cry! . . . All flesh is grass, and all its beauty is like the flower of the field. The grass withers, the flower fades, when the breath of the Lord blows upon it. . . . but the word of our God will stand for ever" (Isa. 40:6-8). What a view: In all the horrible transitoriness under God's wrath, the only reliable thing is the creative word. And how this word acts as a power in the history into which it has entered, Isaiah shows:

> "For as the rain and the snow come down from heaven,
>   and return not thither but water the earth,
> making it bring forth and sprout,
>   giving seed to the sower and bread to the eater,
> so shall my word be that goes forth from my mouth;
>   it shall not return to me empty,
> but it shall accomplish that which I purpose,
>   and prosper in the thing for which I sent it. (55:10-11)

That is certainly the clearest and most basic witness to the creative activity of God's word in history. That word is here like an "accumulation of latent energies" (Grether), that drives history to its judgment and its well-being. What is at stake, therefore, is not the recognition that generally all movements in world history are called forth by Yahweh's word. Nevertheless, in this history a special divine word will set in motion a movement for judgment and salvation, a movement that with sovereign certainty will arrive at its goal. This certainty is a characteristic of the word; it does not fail (Josh. 23:14), it is no "trifle" like an empty nut (Deut. 32:47). God makes the word which has entered history "full" (I Kings 2:27), he "fulfills" it. Another characteristic is the speed with which it works. "He sends forth his command to the earth; his word runs swiftly" (Ps. 147:15). And Habakkuk is dramatic: "I will take my stand to watch . . . and look forth to see what he will say to me, . . . And the Lord answered me: 'Write the vision; make it plain upon tablets. . . . For still the vision awaits its time; it hastens ("pants") to the end—it will not lie. If it seem slow, wait for it; it will surely come' " (2:1-3).

But the matter is not everywhere as clear—as basic, as though formulated for dogmatic theologians—as it is in Second Isaiah. The symbolic acts of the prophets are a chapter in themselves, and they differ markedly from each other in their relationship to the word that is being interpreted. Here I want only to say that scholars today are turning away from the idea that those acts were simply for popular, dramatic demonstration of the prophetic word. Such a conception is too spiritual. They were, rather, actual anticipations of future events; they were creative advance representations in whose wake realization had to follow. They too constituted, then, an effective, molding force in history, which was handed over to the prophets' authority by God.

But there is also the instance in which the prophet interprets history as God's work, where he does not interpolate a word of God into it but receives from God the interpretative word for directly contemporary or past historical events. The prophet can "read" history. The format of Isaiah 18 is overpowering. An Egyptian legation is in Jerusalem. The city is in an uproar as men have watched the tall dark figures go in to the king. Affairs of great moment are being planned on the political stage. Men are drawn into a fever pitch of excitement in which they lose all sense of proportion. At that moment the prophet apprehends a voice from on high. God is enthroned in infinite distance above this human fairground and is waiting. "I will quietly look from my dwelling like clear heat in the sunshine, like a cloud of dew in the heat of harvest. For before the harvest . . . he will cut off the shoots with pruning hooks, and the spreading branches he will hew away." The meaning of the statement is not clear in every detail. God is enthroned in infinite distance above this historical confusion, as on a hot day one can see the heat shimmering at the zenith or the cirrus clouds in the air—but on earth a harvest ripens. God waits, and the hour comes when the luxuriant sprouts of the vine will be pruned, the luxuriant shoots in history. Here the idea of a fulfillment of history—usually the great theme of the prophets—is only obscurely suggested, but for that reason perhaps so impressively. I would like to refer to another text that shows the way a prophet reads history. It is Isaiah 10, the famous chapter on the Assyrians, vv. 5-15. "Ah, Assyria, the rod of my anger, the staff of my fury! Against a godless nation I sent him . . . to take spoil and seize plunder, and to tread them down like the mire of the streets. But he does not so intend, . . . but it is in his mind to destroy, and to cut off nations not a few. . . . Shall the axe vaunt itself over him who hews with it, or the saw magnify itself against him who wields it?" One cannot accept the idea that Assyria actually received a word from Yahweh and in accordance with it undertook a punitive expedition which it then wantonly exceeded. What had the prophet, Isaiah, in mind? I can explain the passage only as the prophet's separation of what for us is hopelessly intertwined, namely, God's working and man's initiative. He sees illuminated in this instance what in the Assyrian attack was God's plan and what should be reckoned to man's sin. He sees—and that means he looks as a true prophet—the difference between the divine plan for history and Assyria's despotism, and he attacks this sin of Assyria that has become revealed to him.

Of course we are not dealing here with an interpretation of general, secular circumstances, but rather with events that occur on the margin of revealed history or are imminently at work in it. Only *this* course of events is set in motion by the Word and molded by constantly renewed words from God that are spoken within it. The other historical events are important only in their relation to this center. Even the most universal of all prophets, Second Isaiah, expressed this one-sided view of salvation as coming exclusively in terms of history. For the nations actually to have received a word from God is a great exception. Yahweh usually deals with them as his instruments in a much more sovereign way. He "awakens" them, or more drastically he whistles for them (Isa. 7:18; 5:26), or he goads a people as though it were a team of oxen (9:10).

Let us return to our problem of the prophet and history. What we saw was a unified thought: the motor, the actual creative power of this history, and this history alone, is God's word. And for that the prophet is given complete authority of interpretation, even where he inserts no word of God into the history. God illuminates the prophets; he gives their spirits access to his Word; therefore they talk about God's plans even where this word has already entered history and itself become part of history. For the history that is formed and created by the word has the power of evidence for the prophets. The Deuteronomistic historical writing in the books of Kings rests upon this presupposition. But of course what we called "Heilsgeschichte" (saving history) is not the golden thread that runs visibly through world history. It is rather a course of events in which God's hiddenness becomes increasingly clear and in which all pious and impious human thoughts go to pieces. Israel ran aground on this history, and it ran aground on God.

But we must amplify this. We spoke of the Word that creates history. Man's part is *faith*. Faith in the Old Testament means entering into this special action of God in history, surrendering oneself to it in confidence and gratitude. That is evident in Genesis 15, where Abraham took seriously what God had promised him. In Isaiah the word about faith takes on a polemical overtone. Here too there is an entering into God's action in history, but there is also something negative involved. Just do not seize God by the arm, do not do anything autocratically. Isaiah tells Ahaz, "Take heed, be quiet!" In Isaiah 7:4 we find the same paradoxical statement about being still that occurs in 30:15. Man in such situations can only come to grief. Therefore, he is to remain completely quiet and not disturb God in his work. Unbelief that does not enter into God's work, that temporizes, stands God aside and lets him wait—unbelief like that wearies God, as Isaiah says with magnificent anthropomorphism (7:13). Such unbelief says neither yea nor nay and thus gets into God's way. This conception of wearying God recurs in Second Isaiah: "You have burdened me with your sins, you have wearied me with your iniquities" (Isa. 43:24; cf. Malachi 2:17).

Wherever this activity of saving history was no longer seen, faith had to go to pieces. We see that in two books,

Job and Ecclesiastes. Both stand in fully nonhistorical space and are there an easy prey for all the demonic temptations that beset our lives. The absence of history is also an absence of community. Thus Job struggles in horrible isolation, as though God had never called a community into being, as though no prophet had ever proclaimed the consummation of history. The author of the ninetieth psalm also seems close to this despair. What does he know of God? He has primarily a depressing conception of God's eternity and of the power of his wrath. And is it not highly significant that in the end he prays that God's works—those in history, of course—and the revelation of God's glory may again be revealed? "Let thy work be manifest to thy servants, and thy glorious power to their children" (v. 16). God is to glorify himself again, to reveal again his work of saving history.

In other circles, however, faith in God's word was passed on from generation to generation. Indeed, a shift in conceptions occurred. Men studied this word so intensively that for those who came later it appeared more and more to stand as something for itself, as something independent and hypostatic alongside God. It was loosed from God's mouth and made a third entity alongside God and man. The Old Testament did not regard the word in this way. There it was like an event that was not to be fixed in flight. Still the passage in the Wisdom of Solomon (18:14-16) about the night of Passover is magnificent: "All things were lying in peace and silence, and night in her swift course was half spent, when thy almighty Word leapt from thy royal throne in heaven into the midst of that doomed land like a relentless warrior, bearing the sharp sword . . . and stood . . . his head touching the heavens, his feet on earth" (NEB).

With that I will leave the subject and add only a few general theological consequences. What I have been telling you are in broad strokes the facts of the matter, the validity of which we have to grant.

Any study of the Old Testament that does not begin

with its character as a witness to God's action in history is condemned to sterility because it does not take account of the facts. Because the Old Testament bears witness to a historical path that God has taken with Israel all the way to Christ, we cannot simply, at will, remove Christ from that context. Old Testament history, in judgment and in salvation, bears witness to *that* action of God that becomes finally revealed in Jesus Christ. Old Testament saving history, brought into being by the word, is thus related to the appearance of the Word in flesh as promise is related to fulfillment. Consider Hebrews 1:1-2. What catches attention in those verses is the conception of a Word that was there to the fathers through the prophets and is here to us through the Son. There is an important consequence of that for every interpretation of scripture and that is the uniform equality of the earliest acts of God in the Old Testament with the Christ event in the New Testament. The judgment and salvation revealed in Jesus Christ are prefigured everywhere in the Old Covenant. That is why we speak about types of Christ in the Old Testament, about prefigurations of what is to come. Thus the Promised Land in the stories of the patriarchs and Moses is an advance figuration of the new life in Christ, and in the patriarchs' relationship to this land are reflected all the temptations and assurances we experience as we await the new salvation granted to us in Christ, except that the fulfillment is always present in the promise. The fulfillment, however, that came with Christ is not final and conclusive, but is itself a promise of the end of the world and the return of the Lord. I refer here to some ideas that O. Schmitz expressed in his article about the Old Testament in the New in the *Heim Festschrift*, they are perhaps the most helpful of any that have been expressed in our time about the question of the Old Testament. Schmitz speaks as follows about the fulfillment of the Old Testament in Jesus Christ.

> This "fulfillment" is not perfection, for the inheritance of the future glory, the redemption of the body is not yet the possession of the heirs. Insofar as they receive spiritually

only an earnest, or pledge of future goods, these goods remain now as before objects of promise. The promise is thus fulfilled "in Christ," but at the same time it is outstanding "with Christ." That is, it will reach whole fulfillment only with his new presence. . . . Thus this pair of conceptions, "Promise" and "fulfillment" contains a strange and ambiguous understanding of the dialectic of saving history . . . a promise that is fulfilled and yet still remains in its fulfillment a promise. It is a fulfillment that leaves the promise far behind and yet as fulfillment becomes another promise." (pp. 65-66)

That means, therefore, that the church of Christ is again on the march from a promise to a fulfillment, and for this reason its situation is analogous to that of the people of the Old Testament. One should remember that Jesus Christ is not present in the flesh with the church, but is with it in the work of the Holy Spirit in history, just as he was also historically present in the Old Covenant. Thus there is repeated in the Christian church the existence of the Old Testament community. The manifold temptations, consolations, judgments, and helps for Israel are also the temptations, consolations, judgments, and helps of the church of Christ; for here as there we have a history effected by the *Word*. This is not, of course, a slavish understanding of the Old Testament, but rather one that is to be fulfilled in the freedom of the Sonship of God in the New Testament. For it has pleased God to go far beyond the promise in many respects in its fulfillment in the New Testament.

Biblical criticism has changed nothing that is of fundamental importance in all of that. We have seen in innumerable instances the much more limited, historically determined sense of the Old Testament witness. One must characterize the dawn of biblical criticism as a wholesome experience for the church, which had become more docetic rather than biblical in its doctrine of Scripture. It had not taken its knowledge about the whole servant form of revelation as seriously as is demanded of us today. But the critical biblical theologians too must stand corrected and learn that the sense of a witness is not to be discovered only from its previous stages in the history of religions; it may be possibly combined with them into one. We have to hear the witness in its final form and see it in its present context. And so far as that is concerned, we can reckon with quite a considerable spiritual content, that is often greatly underestimated, even in the pericopes of the Yahwist and Elohist.

That is one thing. The other that the critics have to learn is much more difficult to formulate scientifically. It happens too often that biblical critics tell us that the completely comprehensive meaning that we are accustomed to derive from a statement of faith in the Old Testament is not there, according to their own understanding of the passage; the meaning is a great deal less comprehensive. Students of Gunkel uncritically spoke and warned against "exceeding" (Überhöhung). Today one may like this admonition, unless the precise meaning (as one said, the incorrect interpretation)—roughly stated, the New Testament meaning—seems much more appropriate for its text. It would be easy to assemble here a whole bundle of statements from the Psalms that simply cry out for this more complete, excessive meaning. What has happened here? Are we simply to say the witnesses took too great a mouthful, chose their words too audaciously? That would not explain precisely the fact that these statements seem to be written for those later, ample contents. The witnesses seem to us like men with jars that are only partially filled with precious content but seem destined at some time to be filled to the brim. Now that is an image and not a theological explanation. The explanation lies in the fact that the witnesses of the Old Covenant had business with the living God and his activity. That explains their radical statements of faith and their orientation toward the whole. These encounters between God and man in the Old Testament tend in their approach to focus on the ultimate and definitive. The extent to which that is invaded by the subjective imagination of the witnesses is probably restricted and temporary; it is also very difficult at times to ascertain. The framework is so universal because the encounters between God and man are always a Christ event. The word that God creatively injects into history, as we have already said, is indeed none other than that which in the fullness of time became flesh.

Here, to be sure, we would have to use more solid theological concepts to lighten the work of the practical interpreter. The material itself, this elasticity of the conceptions of faith in the Old Testament, is open to all eyes. Years ago I tried once to show it in the Old Testament idea of rest. Rest is first of all the end of the conquest of Canaan: God gave his people rest from all their enemies round about. But in the time of the later monarchy, some four hundred years after the conquest, Deuteronomy says, "you have not as yet come to your rest" (12:9). Here the rest is thought of as something still outstanding. In the 95th Psalm God says, "They shall not enter my rest." It is thus God's rest that is offered to the people. Even more daring is Psalm 132, which says that God, with reference to the ark of the covenant, has not yet come to rest on earth with his people. "Arise, O Lord, and go to thy resting place" (v. 8). The way all these strains come together in the book of Hebrews in the witness to God's rest on the seventh day of creation is well-known: "So then, there remains a sabbath rest for the people of God" (4:9). "We who have believed enter that rest" (4:3).

Of course one could cite similar statements of that kind, in a variety of ways, about many terms of faith in the Old Testament. Whether a change in our continued extremely historical exegesis can be affected by studies of such terms alone, I do not know. They would, in any case, have to free themselves completely from every development scheme and then lead to a new conception of saving history in the Old Testament, something that is urgently needed today, just one hundred years after the appearance of Hoffmann's "Prophecy and Fulfillment."

Let me conclude. Our theme is "God's word and history." A second presentation has to follow, "God's word and nature." The first chapter of Genesis bears witness that the whole cosmos owes its existence to the free, creative word of God. If we see the two together, cosmos and history, then a way of understanding is paved for us to the prologue of the Fourth Gospel: "In the beginning was the Word, and the Word was with God, and the Word was God. . . . all things were made through him, and without him was not anything made that was made."

15

THE WITNESS OF THE PROPHETS
TO GOD'S WAYS
IN WORLD HISTORY

(The manuscript of this lecture has neither title nor date; it comes from the 1940s, presumably before 1945. The title suggested above is based on formulations in the lecture itself.)

In light of the terrible inner disintegration and the spiritual cleavage of our people today, we are becoming keenly aware of what our people have lost by ceasing to learn from the Bible and not letting it determine their ideas about God, the world, and man. I am not thinking at all about final consolation in life and in death which it gives us. I mean something more worldly. How much better advised would our fathers and forefathers have been, purely from the viewpoint of education, to have learned to take from the Bible the yardsticks for the things of this world. There are in the Old Testament alone five empires with which the men and writings of ancient Israel came most intensively to grips, and about fourteen centuries have left their mark on our Bible. Its horizon of vision on world history is enormous. It knows about the ancient culture of Egypt; it knows about the astrological world view of Babylon; it is familiar with the colonization of Phoenicians throughout the world. It follows with complete awareness the collapse of a millennium of Semitic domination and sees in the Persians a new era in world history dominated by Indo-Europeans. It also sees the Persian empire fall and the Greek spirit flash with Alexander the Great across the ancient oriental world. It speaks of immeasurably powerful and rich kings and of small, uneducated, and rude commanders of mercenary troops; it draws unforgettable profiles of clever priests or fanatical theologians, of chaste women and of harlots; and in the midst of this confusing world of humanity, the New Testament then shows us the one who is associated as a brother to them all and yet as the most enigmatic stranger, the one of whom the bailiff, who was sent out to arrest him, reported, "Never spoke a man as this one!"

I believe that a person and a people are not badly advised to study this book from their youth onward, to school their thought with it, to take from it their standards in large and small, important and unimportant, matters. No one is so mature and certain about his judgment that he can find his way in the confusion of life alone and unaided, able to distinguish easily between what is important and ultimately decisive and what is of lesser significance. We ourselves today see how quite simple men have maintained breadth of vision and a surety of judgment, in politics too. I would like to say they have genuine education, because they have not allowed their own little world to collapse on itself but have instead kept themselves open constantly to the great world of the Bible.

But for the present we are in general too late for that. Our people have exchanged genuine education for the lentil pottage of a hollow, emancipated, superficial education; and the way that leaves us in the lurch on all worrisome questions is apparent in every newspaper we open. Today what concerns us is no longer education, i.e., special cultural desires, but life itself or despair. What is happening on this earth? What kinds of powers have us in their grasp? Are they the blindly raging powers of chaos that throw us into confusion? Is there any comfort? Who is master in the house of this world and its history? Let me suggest an answer that comes to us from the Old Testament. Do not fear that I am about to burden you with a historical matter which perhaps is quite interesting but has nothing directly to do with our present situation. This answer is of amazingly current importance. Whoever listens to it impartially will ask in astonishment, how is it possible for this old book to know about us and our problems, to mention in detail the enigmas and fears that beset us? But more than that, it knows about something that today has become quite rare.

When the men we call prophets arose in ancient Israel, the nation already had a rather long history behind it. The Israel to which Amos, Isaiah, and Jeremiah spoke was no longer young. On the contrary, the cultural situation was dangerously advanced. Harsh contrasts prevailed in society. A rich and powerful ruling class opposed a deprived proletariat of small landowners, and religious life was torn by severe wrongs. Not that there were many atheists; they had not yet ventured so far. But the life of faith was internally undermined. The altars still smoked; the ancient prayers were still spoken; the words, so to speak, were all there. But behind them there was no serious faith, no true reverence for God. To take this God seriously as the almighty ruler of destiny and human affairs means to worship him in truth as the lord of life and death and to trust him in truth, and that the nation had long since forgotten. Where one turned to God, one thought of him simply as the professional, almost natural dispenser of blessing. What else could be expected of him, then, except to forgive men their sins and guarantee them fullness of life and satisfaction! Is not this picture of such thoughtless, irreverent faith quite familiar to us? It has nothing at all to do with the living God, but is complete idolatry.

In the eleventh century B.C., about the time of Samuel, according to the unambiguous portrayal of the Old Testament sources, there appeared for the first time multitudes of men whom one can liken generally to Islamic dervishes. They were strange bands of ecstatics who crisscrossed the land. The agricultural inhabitants living on their ancestral plots of land did not view them simply as men who were seized and possessed in a strange way by the divine spirit, but rather with derision as madmen. Their appearance was in fact rather strange. Their inspired enthusiasm was not yet capable at this time of commanding articulate statement, and no individual figures emerge into view. Whoever encountered these dancing, stammering, music-making men would have been unable to predict any future for the movement. The prodigious charisma with which God had endowed them was still asleep.

Two hundred years later the picture is completely different. Then we find communities of prophets at the shrines, men assembled around a leader like Elisha almost in the manner of congregations of monks. Those circles were indeed very poor economically, almost declassed one might say; and one can ask whether those who joined them did not thereby firmly close the door behind them to social acceptance.

Another hundred years later, about the middle of the eighth century, we encounter the first of the so-called great prophets: Amos, Hosea, Isaiah, and Micah. We must not imagine them, however, as the towering leaders to whom the great number of less important prophets were attached and whom they followed. On the contrary, they were outsiders who at times took a strong stand against a prophetic status that was stratified, professionally consolidated, and, one might almost say, official. There is still much we do not know about the special, traditional circles and educational forces that influenced the growth of these groups and their message. That is because these men speak with a unique intransigence about the message that is committed to them. They themselves, their entire subjective lives with their fortunes, stand in the shadows of those objective commissions. And these messages, often received by revelation in the midst of suffering that burdened the psyche to the limit of the endurable, contained no metaphysical disclosures or knowledge of higher worlds; instead they are concerned totally with affairs that are fully immanent in history. The prophets impart the plans and historical intentions of God to a generation, to be sure, that in large measure has lost the ability to be amazed or shocked at the staggering new perspectives. No one trained himself to be a prophet; the calling is not to be understood as the process of slow inner maturing. "The lion has roared; who will not fear? The Lord God has spoken; who can but prophesy?" (Amos 3:8). From then on the speech and thought of these men was subject to completely different laws. They paid no attention to what troubled others as a whole. Where those others lived quietly and confidently, the prophets excited them with frightful vision; where men speak and fly into passion, the prophets remain silent and unruffled; and where men are silent and satisfied, the prophets raise their voices in cries of woe whose echo carries across the centuries to our ears.

When the high priest at Bethel in c. 750 B.C. heard about the coming of Amos and his preaching, he sent a report to the king, as a good official would, with his own recommendation: "the land is not able to bear all his words" (Amos 7:10). What did he mean by that? I think the statement came from an attentive observer. Apparently he wants to say that the preaching of this Amos calls into question everything that the good and devout people throughout the land are thinking and speaking about God. That high priest was no fool; he had a very clear perception of the enormity of the prophetic message; he actually found himself somewhat addressed by it. And we could say the same thing about king Ahab, who called Elijah a "troubler of Israel" (I Kings 18:17). Hosea had to let himself be called a fool, and Jeremiah had the same experience when he wrote that wonderful pastoral letter to the exiles. We want to take these indications quite seriously. It seems probable that these prophets would experience the same thing today, for their message was intolerable to the ears of the religious.

At the time of the prophet Isaiah in 735 a tangled situation involving efforts at political coalition prevailed. "In that day the Lord will whistle for the fly . . . of Egypt, and for the bee . . . of Assyria" (Isa. 7:18). God summons world empires, as a man whistles for an animal. They stand ready at once to serve him, against his own people and nation. Assyria and Egypt! The devout Israelite thought that God would some day destroy these enemies of his people. But the prophet said that God summoned them against his people as the instrument of his judgment (Isa. 7:19). In the next verse we read: "In that day the Lord will shave with a razor which is hired beyond the River . . . the head and the hair of the feet, and it will sweep away the beard also" (7:20). God the Barber! He hires a razor and then shaves everything clean. Is it fitting to speak about God like this? But what is remarkable is the way the proportions are shifted for the prophets! When an empire appears in our historical field of vision, it takes up all the space; all thoughts are directed toward it, and God who is at work in the background seems to us shadowy and uncertain. For us to define God's relationship to and activity with this world power and its activity taxes our sense perception with insuperable difficulties. Just the opposite is true of the prophets! That empire beyond the Euphrates is nothing at all; it is a borrowed razor, nothing more. It exists as though it had no will of its own, no power of self-motivation; all activity proceeds from God. Men see an empire which they do not know to be dangerous or not; the prophet sees only God, and God quite directly and immediately at work in history! To see that way is to see prophetically.

We have another example. God speaks through the mouth of the prophet Hosea, "I am like a moth to Ephraim, and like dry rot to the house of Judah" (Hos. 5:12). God a moth to Israel? Has the man taken leave of his senses? But the prophet sees what no one else sees. The citizens would perhaps have admitted that the nation was suffering from social, economic, or other ills. But Hosea sees quite differently. The nation is sick with God! And what fools they are that look for help from great diplomacy or from any new constellation of treaties, "When Ephraim saw his sickness, and Judah his wound, then Ephraim went to Assyria, and sent to the great king. But he is not able to cure you or heal your wound" (Hos. 5:13). What is staggering in this vision is the directness and immediacy with which these men see God ruling over history. For them contemporary historical events do not obstruct their view of God, as they do for us, so that behind all the confusion on the stage of history God can perhaps be perceived as a possibility of a problem. Their order of precedence is the reverse. They see God filling all history with his rule; and contemporary affairs, that for us obstruct the sight of God, for them shrivel to almost nothing.

But there is something else that is more important. The God, whose footprint in history the prophets have been permitted to recognize, is a hidden God, much more hidden than the upright, devout souls, their contemporaries, were willing to admit. "My thoughts are not your thoughts, neither are your ways my ways," says the prophet in the light of God's contemporary acts in history; "for as the heavens are higher than the earth, so are my ways higher than your ways and my thoughts than your thoughts" (Isa. 55:8-9). The prophets thus stand in fierce conflict with the views of the devout men of their time. For it is the naively religious person who is tempted to control God, to make God in his own image. But such a person, often enough the devout person, is then dealing not with the living God but rather with a sophisticated reflection of his own ideas of God. We see these prophets, therefore, widely engaged in striking the idol of God as a well-meaning sovereign from the hands of their contemporaries. Man with his limited understanding has no clue to this God's plans and ideas for history, least of all when he thinks "God must" or "God could not." And once God makes a person privy to his plans, that person experiences what happened to the prophet Ezekiel who sat dazed and in bitter indignation for seven days. What a shudder must have gone through those Jerusalemites when Isaiah spoke before them his message about the strange and unfamiliar work of God that later became so important to Luther: "For the Lord will rise up as on Mount Perazim, he will be wroth as in the valley of Gibeon; to do his deed—strange is his deed! and to work his work—alien is his work!" (Isa. 28:21).

Now Isaiah's contemporaries had, of course, their own conception of history. They expected great things in it. So diplomacy continued on high levels, envoys hurried between states, far-reaching alliances were to be formed, and affairs of great moment were in the offing. But, it was revealed to Isaiah, God had nothing to do with this activity. As distant as the stars he sits enthroned above this annual fair of diplomacy: "I will quietly look from my dwelling like clear heat in sunshine, like a cloud of dew in the heat of harvest" (Isa. 18:4). It is a wonderful vision. As one sees so far and high on a summer's day the clear, shimmering heat at the zenith or the filmy veil of a cloud of dew hovering over the earth, so God sits enthroned worlds above the confusion of history. But he waits, for on earth the harvest approaches: "For before the harvest, when the blossom is over, and the flower becomes a ripening grape, he will cut off the shoots with pruning hooks, and the spreading branches he will hew away" (Isa. 18:5). It is the image of a vineyard. When the time comes, the great, divine Vintner will go to work and cut away the shoots of the vines, the rank growth of history! And then the prophet shows with wonderful sarcasm how all the trimmings will be thrown on the dump, where beasts perhaps have their lairs (Isa. 18:6). What a contrast: on earth unrest, the mood for political sensationalism—above the unending calm of the Lord of history!

If we reflect a moment, we will realize that we have now heard two sounds from the prophetic proclamation:

1) God's power in history is complete. He is decisively at work in everything. Nations and empires that seem so totally dominating to us are nothing before him. "Behold, the nations are like a drop from the bucket, and are accounted as dust on the scales" (Isa. 40:15).

2) But God's sovereignty in history is hidden; it mocks the most clever and profound human criteria and confronts man with imponetrable riddles. But in that which seems senseless to man, like an agonizing round of affairs, God is mobilizing history for his great future. That was, indeed, one of the most remarkable illuminations of the prophets, that in the midst of a generation that was indifferent to and secure in this flow, this stream of history, they were given to perceive its end, the Day of the Lord. Much in history contradicts God's will, but God

comes. He does not intend to liquidate his creation; he comes to establish his kingdom.

I must trouble you here with a consideration of interest purely to the history of religions: The world outlook of the entire ancient Near East was characterized by a mythical, cyclical view of events that dominated the sacred and cultic as well as the profane. This all-encompassing view, that gave order to the world, arose from contemplation of the return of the stars each night. From that were derived the great cosmic orders in which all divine and human events had their origin. The year rose and fell, and the aeons of the world likewise rolled on in powerful cycles from cosmos to chaos to cosmos. Thus for Hesiod the aeons decline from golden to iron ages and then issue in their original state. Similarly, Greek history was not characterized by the teleological idea that is so familiar to us. "The historical world and historical time, as we know them, were unknown to the ancient world" (K. Reinhardt) Something of this unhistorical quality is common to all ancient and modern mythologies.

This ancient Near Eastern, mythological, essentially unhistorical view of the world is as far from prophetic historical thinking as fire is from water. The prophets do not share a mythical view of eternal return, but see, rather, the events of the deity with the world as a single, unrolling, never reversible course. This end toward which the prophets look is in some way God's self-realization in the world, be it in the court of his holiness, in the establishment of his lordship over the nations, in the coming of his representative, the anointed one. It is thus, in any case, the end of the present indirect relationship of man to God.

From the viewpoint of the history of religion we have a strange picture: that majestic, ancient Near Eastern, mythical picture of the world that arose in and went forth from the ancient cultures of Mesopotamia and was freely accepted by the surrounding peoples and cultures was strictly rejected by a small, provincial nation. Was it not tremendous audacity for them to emancipate themselves from this cosmological order on which millennia had built? What reason was there to dispute the divine rank of those siderial powers? Did not Israel see the world dissolve into chaos as she smashed this wholesome world order that had been reverently accepted since antiquity? What did she have to put in its place? What ordering power made the world and its history seem to her a unit, a cosmos, guided by God? It was simply her belief in God's total power in history and her knowledge that history is moving toward the great manifestation of God in history.

One has the impression that the prophets were under the influence of this future event as though under a spell, as though there streamed from it a frightful fluid that struck these men physically with a mad suspense. How else should we understand Zephaniah's lament over the approaching day of the Lord? "The great day of the Lord is near, near and hastening fast; the sound of the day of the Lord is bitter, the mighty man cries aloud there. A day of wrath is that day, a day of distress and anguish, . . . a day of darkness and gloom, . . . a day of trumpet blast" (Zeph. 1:14-16). This day, this coming of God in history, will reveal first what's up with mankind. Then all vainglory will break to pieces, and what men previously worshiped and considered great will be known to be hollow and ridiculous. Let me read a few verses from Isaiah's overpoweringly magnificent hymn about this coming of God:

> Enter into the rock,
>   and hide in the dust
> from before the terror of the LORD,
>   and from the glory of his majesty.
> The haughty looks of man shall be brought low,
>   and the pride of men shall be humbled;
> and the LORD alone will be exalted in that day.
> For the LORD of hosts has a day
>   against all that is proud and lofty,
>   against all that is lifted up and high;
> against all the cedars of Lebanon,
>   lofty and lifted up;
>   and against all the oaks of Bashan;
> against all the high mountains,
>   and against all the lofty hills;

against every high tower,
    and against every fortified wall;
against all the ships of Tarshish,
    and against all the beautiful craft.
And the haughtiness of man shall be humbled,
    and the pride of men shall be brought low;
and the LORD alone will be exalted in that day.
And the idols shall utterly pass away.
And men shall enter the caves of the rocks
    and the holes of the ground,
from before the terror of the LORD,
    and from the glory of his majesty,
    when he rises to terrify the earth.
In that day men will cast forth
    their idols of silver and their idols of gold,
which they made for themselves to worship,
    to the moles and to the bats,
to enter the caverns of the rocks
    and the clefts of the cliffs,
from before the terror of the LORD,
    and from the glory of his majesty,
    when he rises to terrify the earth. (Isa. 2:10-21)

That is the message of the prophets about the great breakdown toward which all history streams. But now it has to be said that these men placed themselves first and foremost under the judgment of the breakdown. They became poor, lonely, indeed ridiculed, spit upon, and beaten; and in that they did not proudly preserve their souls in philosophical immovability. No, they participated in the suffering and let it flood over them; step by step they descended into the night of God-forsakenness and walked the road on which Jesus Christ, on the night in which he was betrayed, descended into the lowest depths of darkness and God-forsakenness.

In Jeremiah we see how the way of his poor life descends more and more steeply into suffering and despair.

"The harvest is past, the summer is ended,
    and we are not saved."
For the wound of the daughter of my people is my heart
    wounded,
    I mourn, and dismay has taken hold on me.

Is there no balm in Gilead?
    Is there no physician there?
Why then has the health of the daughter of my people
    not been restored?
    O that my head were waters,
and my eyes a fountain of tears. (Jer. 8:20-22–9:1)

This too is part of the great breakdown toward which history is hastening, this shattering of the prophets on God. Jeremiah reports that he once complained to God that for himself the problems associated with God's direction of the world were too difficult, too opaque; the actual events of history mock all explanations.

Righteous art thou, O LORD,
    when I complain to thee;
  yet I would plead my case before thee.
Why does the way of the wicked prosper?
    Why do all who are treacherous thrive?
Thou plantest them, and they take root;
    they grow and bring forth fruit;
thou art near in their mouth
    and far from their heart.
But thou, O LORD, knowest me;
    thou seest me, and triest my mind toward thee.
Pull them out like sheep for the slaughter,
    and set them apart for the day of slaughter.
How long will the land mourn,
    and the grass of every field wither?
For the wickedness of those who dwell in it
    the beasts and the birds are swept away,
    because men said, "He will not see our latter end."
"If you have raced with men on foot,
        and they have wearied you,
    how will you compete with horses?
And if in a safe land you fall down,
    how will you do in the jungle of the Jordan?" (Jer. 12:1-5)

A strange answer that contains no clarification! On the contrary, behind the curtain that conceals history there are no solutions but instead many much darker problems about which men have no inkling. God says to Jeremiah, Are you so without a clue about the true backgrounds of history? Do you really believe that the divine solution to what is troubling you lies in what you have said? And precisely that was Jeremiah's task, to go out into this darkness.

The scene Jeremiah shows us is touching. He has his faithful scribe, Baruch, write down in a book all the frightful prophecies, and the scribe groans and puts away his pen. He can write no more. But Jeremiah gives him a strong and yet gracious word from God. "Behold, what I have built I am breaking down, and what I have planted I am plucking up—that is, the whole land. And do you seek great things for yourself? Seek them not; for behold, I am bringing evil upon all flesh, says the Lord; but I will give you your life as a prize of war in all places to which you may go" (Jer. 45:4-5). Your life as a prize of war? Is the breakdown not yet the final one; beyond the judgment is there something else? Beyond anger is there life? Yes, it is evidently true! God wills salvation for this man condemned to dust, this man whose criteria for great and small have been broken and whose idols have been smashed.

With that we touch on the greatest mystery of the prophets' message, and, in the circle of Old Testament study, the question that has attracted endless debate, How it is thinkable at all that these men should have prophesied salvation? Indeed, we really do not know how to answer that question. But the prophets did announce salvation, and therein they made us very old promises that had been given to ancient Israel. God will bless Israel, and in her all generations on earth shall be blessed; Israel is only the point of entry for a salvation that will reach far beyond the limits of the Old Testament covenant people to include the world. That was the hope of salvation handed on from the patriarchal era. But what was only an occasional sound in a lonely word of prophecy in that early period, is taken up in time by the prophets in fuller and fuller tones.

I said that the shrill message of judgment and the more and more full and comforting proclamation of salvation are difficult to comprehend in their juxtaposition and interplay. One thing, however, is clear: Here it is revealed to man that God can speak his yes only after he has spoken a no. Only by means of that great breakdown in world history can God's work be revealed, a work that he has already begun in great secrecy. God has already laid the foundation in this historical period of ours for his coming kingdom; he has determined a place of refuge, of comfort, and of hope, hidden still from the eyes of the great world and known only to a small nation of those who believe and are chosen. "Behold, I am laying in Zion for a foundation a stone, a tested stone, a precious cornerstone, of a sure foundation: 'He who believes will not be in haste' " (Isa. 28:16). And this place, where God has laid his salvation, the only place in this world to which man is invited so that protection and grace from above may encompass him, since man will not outlive his deadly disorder—this place is exposed without any visible protection to the frightful powers that do their work on the field of history. No power, that could compete in any way with the power of the nations, protects it. It appears to be delivered unarmed before the charges of the powers of the abyss. But that is only an appearance. God has reserved the role of protector to himself. "Not by might, nor by power, but by my Spirit, says the Lord of hosts" (Zech. 4:6). Again and again the unbelieving believers have thought they had to defend Zion with earthly measures of security like military armaments or the clever politics of alliances. Isaiah creates a gripping scene when he turns aside the diplomatic deputation of foreign nations with a wonderfully sovereign gesture: "What will one answer the messengers of the nation? 'The Lord has founded Zion, and in her the afflicted of his people find refuge' " (Isa. 14:32).

But when the great and bitter breakdown of the Tower of Babel in human history comes, then the place where God has laid his salvation will remain; it will remain when everything else collapses and falls. "Lift up your eyes to the heavens, and look at the earth beneath; for the heavens will vanish like smoke, the earth will wear out like a garment, and they who dwell in it will die like gnats; but my salvation will be for ever, and my deliverance will never be ended" (Isa. 51:6). And there is more: only then will the place that until then has been abandoned defenseless to persecution, denial, despair, and mockery be revealed in glory. Then when the mountain of God, which is now insignificant, is brought out of its ambiguity and revealed to the whole world in glory, as Isaiah 2 tells us in an apocalyptic vision, all nations will flow to it, because in their search for peace they will no longer be able to help it. And then they will beat their swords into plowshares and their spears into pruning hooks (Isa. 2:2-4). In another passage in Isaiah this final glory of God before the nations is prophesied in such a wonderful and consolatory way that it is scarcely surpassed by any other prophetic statement from the Old Testament: God "will destroy on this mountain (Zion) the covering that is cast over all peoples, the veil that is spread over all nations. He will swallow up death for ever, and the Lord God will wipe away tears from all faces, and the reproach of his people he will take away from all the earth; for the Lord has spoken (Isa. 25:7-8).

I come to the end. Is it not true that to see history in this way, to see God's concealed sovereignty in it and its flow toward the great breakdown, is not a matter of a particular philosophy of history? It is not a possibility of human perspicacity or profundity; it is not a general truth that lies tangibly in history to be recognized by anyone who has the will to do so. Plainly stated, that perception can be only a gift of illumination, of a special revelation in which God grants us himself. For that reason we can never read and understand all these statements and this enormous history without thinking of our Lord Jesus Christ, for they are all concerned only with him and his appearance in the world, and with the light that falls on our world with his coming. When we were speaking earlier about the one place of salvation, about its defenseless surrender and eventual glorification at the end of time, who did not think of Jesus Christ? And if these connections are still not clear to anyone, let him see one last prophetic passage. It is the one about the suffering servant of God, who bore our sickness and our pains and was broken for our sins so that we might have peace. The figure of this one homely, impotent, perishing servant of God is portrayed by the prophet in the broadest thinkable framework. The prophet places the entire world of nations, all of mankind together with all their kings, opposite him, precisely at the moment when they realize what they have to do with this servant of God:

> Behold, my servant shall prosper,
>   he shall be exalted and lifted up,
>   and shall be very high.
> As many were astonished at him—
>   his appearance was so marred, beyond human
>   semblance,
>   and his form beyond that of the sons of men—
> so shall he startle many nations;
>   kings shall shut their mouths because of him;
>   for that which has not been told them they shall see,
>   and that which they have not heard they shall
>   understand. (Isa. 52:13-15)

That is the end of God's ways in the history of the world as the prophets of the Old Covenant saw it.

16

WISDOM IN ISRAEL

(Lecture on North German Radio, February 1970.)

What do we mean when we say of a man that he is wise? There are men who know a frightful amount and are not wise at all, and there are those who are completely untaught at whose wisdom we wonder. Wisdom apparently is not a matter of knowing many facts but rather of knowing about man, about life, and also about God. It is a knowing which one embraces and which one lives. Wisdom has many possibilities of expression. A quite hidden gesture can express wisdom, and silence has long been a special prerogative of the wise. But of course her highest and noblest expression has been in word, especially the proverb, the judicious statement, and the maxim.

Ancient Israel took pains in a way all her own to cultivate such proverbial wisdom and to preserve its yield, carefully sifted, in comprehensive collections of proverbs. Her concern was not with a philosophy nor with the solution of ultimate questions about man and the world. Rather, I almost said "on the contrary," she was interested in the near-at-hand and the routine, about trivial questions of succeeding and failing, about good and bad experiences which one has during the day, between morning and evening. Basically she was interested in what everyone knows and no one fathoms. Is not this where the biggest riddles arise?

This is the province of the wise man. He listens

intensely out there in the apparent confusion of daily experience; he observes precisely human reactions; he ponders his own action particularly and the sudden opportunities that come to him. And he concludes that one can learn an astounding amount from what happens to people about us and what we ourselves experience. That is not at all senseless. Rules are operative there, and regulations can be known. Necessities are taken care of, and one needs only patience and open eyes. Thus we read: "For everything there is a season, and a time for every matter under heaven" (Eccles. 3:1-8).

To begin with, we all know that human experience is not always equally successful and meaningful. The warrant for meaningful action is tied to definite times. To know them seemed to the ancients worthy of intense reflection. At first that looks like an uncomfortable statement. But whoever perceives behind it something like a regulation of affairs and whoever knows about the appropriate time for a matter can draw useful consequences; he can allow the right time to carry him to his goal. That is true for all of life, but nowhere so importantly as in speech, in the use of words. An unbelievable importance attaches to saying the right word at the right time. Listen: "A word fitly spoken is like apples of gold in a setting of silver" (Prov. 25:11). The word by itself, however correct it may be, is not enough. But when it falls into the right situation it has its effect, and something beautiful has happened.

Just as the wise men, in their teaching about correct timing, paid close attention to all events, so also they asked about the reasons for hindrances and failures as well as visible blessing. They were profoundly convinced that there is an order in things. Even though man cannot quite take its measure, it cannot be kept secret from him. The world is not a hieroglyph for man. He can read from it; indeed he has to if he wants to get through life. One can understand that especially great catastrophes in the life of an individual, financial ruin, for example, provided food for constant reflection. That indolence brings penury is obvious. But perhaps there was more to it than that. An inner disorder perhaps? Listen: "When pride comes, then comes disgrace; . . . pride goes before destruction, and a haughty spirit before a fall" (Prov. 11:2; 16:18). Proverbs like those are not, of course, general recipes. They say, rather, "think it over; there is much truth in it."

And now let me say something about fools, about whom there is so much written in the book of Proverbs. Foolishness is not, of course, a lack of intelligence. Foolishness is a disorder in a person's deepest being; that is why it says, "the heart of a fool is not right" (von Rad). "The lips of the wise spread knowledge; not so the minds of fools" (Prov. 15:7). He is unable to adapt to the secretly sovereign orders. Mostly there is something without any sense of proportion in him; he overestimates himself. Indeed he wrongs himself. Thus we read that the fool rages against God (Prov. 19:3). Wisdom is not simply knowledge of a subject, we said. It is almost more a trait of character than of intellect; especially is it a matter of trust, indeed, let us say it directly, of faith. Clearly, good sense and faith are united in a highly positive way in the wise person. How deeply her wisdom was rooted in faith Israel knew quite clearly. The fear of the Lord is the beginning of wisdom (Prov. 1:7). Only when we put away all apparent familiarity with this rather well-worn statement do we detect how this maxim encompasses the result of a long process of thought in the extraordinary compactness of a single statement. The beginning, the starting point of every striving for wisdom is knowledge of God. There is no knowing that does not cast the knower quickly back to the question about his knowledge and understanding of himself. The wise men in Israel knew that all possibility of and warrant for knowledge began with the question about a man's relationship to God. Thus the statement that the relationship to God is the beginning of wisdom is a statement of penetrating insight. Only the knowledge about God and about his sovereign rule puts a man in the proper relationship to the objects of his knowledge. Faith does not impede knowing. On the contrary, it sets it free and lets it get down to business. Evidently knowing has felt comfortable in close proximity with faith.

Earlier research on Israelite wisdom was devoted principally to maxims that speak about God or deal with religious questions. Today, however, we are more interested in those that do not speak that way but are formulated about worldly questions, because we are beginning to understand this worldliness in which the wise men saw things as distinct from what we now all call secular. Theirs is the total worldliness of a world that is totally grasped by God. In saying that, we have for the first time defined the magnetic field within which the thought of the wise men was actively at work. Whatever happened to man in this life—delimited and ruled by God—the wise men considered carefully and asked whether perhaps some regularity of occurrence might not be inferred from it. With it belonged also God's activity that is inseparably enmeshed in every event. Were then God's blessing or his denial not experiences? Did they not also provoke the will to know? To be sure, our contemporary scientific customs are different. Nevertheless the ancients have an advantage in practical wisdom, and we ought not be too good to sit at their feet. Listen: "The plans of the mind belong to man, but the answer of the tongue is from the Lord" (Prov. 16:1).

Here heart and tongue are set in a remarkable contrast, in fact, as regions in which the contrast between man and God under some circumstances is particularly clearly recognizable. "The plans of the mind belong to man." What is meant is the restless devising of plans, the inexhaustible advance planning of every conceivable project. Man does that; that is his field in which he is master. But that is not all. The schemes of his mind come to nothing. What is decisive is the way man can make them valid in the word. And that is what the wise men are saying. The road from the restlessly considered project to the word, to the good, appropriate, and cogent word, to the timely word, is broad; and much can happen on the way, over which one has absolutely no control. Therefore be aware that God is precisely in the midst of those imponderables, and in one stroke, of which you have yet to notice anything, he will take the whole matter out of your hand. The same idea occurs in another passage: "A man's mind plans his way, but the Lord directs his steps" (Prov. 16:9).

Do not understand that as an expression of a strong faith in God. It comes rather from the very sober experience of men who undertook to master life and all its potentialities and in the process hit against limits. The passage expresses the wonder of men who have seen again and again how a matter that they thought they had firmly in hand turned imperceptibly and went in another direction. And these limits that they hit over and over again were signs to them that they had a rich playing field for their wills, but that they should never surrender to the delusion that they were sovereign lords of their lives.

When we talk about experiencing limits, we tend today to think primarily negatively, to see something that interrupts human activity. But when the ancients put their minds to understand the mystery that lies between human planning and the actual realization of those plans, and when they saw there a particular field for God's providence, then these limits appeared in a different light. Were they not to be considered as something beneficial? Could there not, equally well, be seen in that which man feels is a limit God's providential care which guards man against his own follies and does not abandon him to his human wisdom about limits? Knowledge about the divine presence in all human activity, now setting a limit to man's plans, now carrying them far beyond the stated goal, was ultimately comforting. So I can now give you one of the most radical statements thinkable, without having to fear that you can detect in it anything like a resigned attitude of the will-to-knowledge whose wings have been broken. Listen: "No wisdom, no understanding, no counsel, can avail against the Lord. The horse is made ready for the day of battle, but the victory belongs to the Lord" (Prov. 21:30-31).

In this astonishing maxim, knowledge about limits is formulated in an especially radical way. The maxim becomes particularly astonishing when one realizes that it does not intend to admonish man about the acquisition and use of wisdom. Its intention was only to guard against the error that there is a guarantee for success in mustering the most superior human wisdom. A person must always remain ready for the act of God that is completely excluded from every reckoning. There is always a great unknown between the mustering of the most reliable wisdom and what then finally happens; it is a gulf which the most realistic knowledge of life is unable to bridge.

Israel, however, knew also that this shattering of all human wisdom can come as a frightful judgment on man. The prophet Isaiah once saw a time drawing near to his people when God would condemn all the wisdom of the wise to impotence. Events will come before which the discernment of the discerning must hide. A night will come for which human understanding and human interpretation are no longer a match. Listen: "Therefore, behold, I will again do marvelous things with this people, wonderful and marvelous; and the wisdom of their wise men shall perish, and the discernment of their discerning men shall be hid" (Isa. 29:14).

Let us summarize. Israel's wise men began with the conviction that there is an order in things, and they therefore pushed their students into the fight between making and losing sense. Only a fool will dispense, to his own disadvantage, with trying to overhear those regulations that support life. But the fight is not won with the will to knowledge only. All knowledge about the world and man begins with knowledge about God. The fear of the Lord, knowledge about God, is the beginning of all wisdom. It is never true that the world refuses when we ask it about God and his rule. On the contrary, it becomes at once both quite real and mysterious only in the light of this question. I see the actual achievement of these wise men in their awareness, with wide-awake common sense, that this world is governed through and through by God. Only when one begins with that awareness, i.e., from this openness to the world and to God, will one understand one of the most profound of Israel's insights: the truly wise person is only the one who thinks himself not wise. To think of oneself as wise is a sure sign of foolishness.

Neglect of wisdom would be the last reproach one could make against these teachers, but they drew limits with astonishing rigor. Wisdom itself can never be the object of trust or the final support of life. Jeremiah said it best: "Let not the wise man glory in his wisdom, let not the mighty man glory in his might, let not the rich man glory in his riches; but let him who glories glory in this, that he understands and knows me, that I am the Lord" (Jer. 9:23-24).

17

BROTHER AND NEIGHBOR IN THE OLD TESTAMENT

(Undated typescript.)

The story of Cain and Abel is the doorway to all of the remarks that follow. It belongs to the biblical primeval history, i.e., its intent is to sketch the image of man, to present something generally valid about his nature. This postparadisial man was a murderer of his brother from the start. He is murderer not only when he forgets himself and sinks into the realm of the subhuman, i.e., when he shows himself as a felon in the criminal sense of the word, but also at the altar where he rises to worship. He envies his brother for God's friendly regard of him; he envies him his share in God. That is certainly the most frightful denial of brotherhood. Even more, he disregards God's question about his brother. He throws off the question, where is your brother Abel, with an impudent pun: Shall I shepherd the shepherd? Now the narrative shows that this is the cause of man's awful homelessness and unrest. Man was taken from the earth, the earth was the motherly base of his life; but now this solidarity between man and earth is destroyed. Man has become homeless on the earth.

That is the first word of the Old Testament about our theme, and everything that follows will have to be understood more or less from this background. The picture of primeval history is a pessimistic one. The history of mankind with God is a history of greater and greater catastrophes. But God has revealed himself to Israel; he has chosen her. That is not a presumptuous theological theory. Rather, Israel simply found herself directly in the equally threatening and cheering presence of Yahweh. Yahweh made Israel the object of his plans in history; he promised to support her through history, to protect and bless her. It is clear that this clasp by God gives to human relationship, i.e., to human neighborliness, its particular character. It has been said correctly that Israel did not become a nation by natural, i.e., by historically biological means, but rather that she experienced her national status on the basis of an alleged community of worship (amphictyony). The common faith in Yahweh, not primarily historical presuppositions of kinship, was the bond that held Israel together. We expect, therefore, to find in the Old Testament very specific statements about brotherhood, which have been stamped by Israel's faith. We order them in two major groups: I. The helpless brother, and II. The wayward brother.

I

The Old Testament presents imposing and widely extended social legislation. These parts of the Old Testament are set forth in many generally understandable texts, and much has been said in praise of these laws. The mass of material may therefore be suggested very briefly.

Legislation about slaves (Exod. 21:1 ff.; Deut. 15). A tenth for the needy (Deut. 14:28 f.). Limits to liens (Exod. 22:25 f.; Deut. 24:6, 10 ff.). Gleaning for the poor (Lev. 19:9 f.; Deut. 24:21). Obligation to provide relief for the poor (Lev. 25:35). Theft of food (Deut. 23:25 f.). Sabbath observance (Exod. 23:12; Deut. 5:14), etc.

I would like to express two feelings about this legislation, first one that is generally human and then one that is theological. One can really only marvel at the social impetus that impels these laws. When we compare them with non-Israelite legal statements from the ancient Near East, we are often able point by point to establish the superiority of these legal statements in the social realm.

Israel took pains to achieve the legal equality of everyone before the law. The stranger, the poor person, and the slave were to enjoy the benefit of legal security. But there is an uncertain ring to this praise of ours. This legislation sometimes seemed just like a magnanimous anticipation of the most ideal humanitarian efforts of modern times. But that particularly is very wrong. All social programs, ever since the Enlightenment, have been concerned with the human right to happiness, a person's legitimate claim to the good things of this life, etc. These regulations from the Old Testament, however, are not concerned with man but with God. Not because man is so worthy or because he has inalienable rights, but because God does not will it; therefore the poor may not be exploited nor the orphan wronged when judgments are handed down. All our modern humanitarian socialism is but an expression of human self-assertion. I just said, because Yahweh does not will it. Why not? Because, as the book of Deuteronomy says again and again, he loves Israel. Now that is quite a different basis from any the most noble socialism can provide. To express it differently, this eminently brotherly legislation is to be understood not as human law or natural right, nor even as law of the state, but rather as regulation for community. There is a good example of it in the so-called dodecalogue of Shechem: "Cursed be the man who makes a graven or molten image. . . . Cursed be he who dishonors his father or his mother. . . . Cursed be he who removes his neighbor's landmark. . . . Cursed be he who misleads a blind man on the road. . . . Cursed be he who perverts the justice due to the sojourner, the fatherless, and the widow" (Deut. 27:15-19).

This series of commands is to be understood only liturgically. It belongs in the middle of a festal ceremony of the community. The statements that are here quoted in part have one thing in common: they are against crimes that could be committed in secret, out of public view. But the community knows that Yahweh's will for justice reaches into the most secret realms, even where the eye of an earthly witness never looks. Here, then, it is fully clear that these statements are not social legislation in which man is talking ultimately about himself, but rather that God claims community as his concern and proclaims his sovereign right over it.

Take another example that shows that these commands derive from the religious rites. It is the beautiful series in Leviticus 19:13 ff.

> "You shall not oppress your neighbor or rob him. The wages of a hired servant shall not remain with you all night until the morning. You shall not curse the deaf or put a stumbling block before the blind, (but you shall fear your God): . . .
> "You shall do no injustice in judgment; you shall not be partial to the poor or defer to the great, (but in righteousness shall you judge your neighbor). You shall not go up and down as a slanderer among your people. . . .
> "You shall not hate your brother in your heart, (but you shall reason with your neighbor, lest you bear sin because of him). You shall not take vengeance or bear any grudge against the sons of your own people, (but you shall love your neighbor as yourself.)" (vv. 13-18)

This series too was once liturgical; the clauses in parentheses are doubtless later additions and theologically interesting as such, because they transpose the ancient negative formulation into a positive one. In other words, a later age on its own authority interpreted the ancient command productively. As a final example of such series of cultic commands, consider the great mirror of confession in Job 31.

> "I have made a covenant with my eyes;
> how then could I look upon a virgin? . . .
> "If I have walked with falsehood,
> and my foot has hastened to deceit; . . .
> if my step has turned aside from the way
> and my heart has gone after my eyes. . . .
> "If my heart has been enticed to a woman,
> and I have lain in wait at my neighbor's door;
> then. . . .
> "If I have rejected the cause of my manservant or my
> maidservant, . . .
> "If I have withheld anything that the poor desired,
> or have caused the eyes of the widow to fail,

or have eaten my morsel alone, . . .
if I have seen any one perish for lack of clothing,
  or a poor man without covering; . . .
if I have raised my hand against the fatherless,
  because I saw help in the gate; . . .
"If I have made gold my trust,
  or called fine gold my confidence;
if I have rejoiced because my wealth was great,
  or because my hand had gotten much;
if I have looked at the sun when it shone,
  or the moon moving in splendor,
and my heart has been secretly enticed,
  and my mouth has kissed my hand; . . .
"If I have rejoiced at the ruin of him that hated me,
  or exulted when evil overtook him. . . ." (vv. 1-29)

An insignificant detail in that wonderful document should give us occasion for a theological consideration. The command in verse 15 rests apparently on belief in the creation. Now in the realm of the Old Testament that is something new and surprising. In the theology of Deuteronomy (see 5:14-15) we find an argumentation that was much more common in Israel, namely, that the day of rest is dedicated to God. Thus there shall be no work on that day for manservant or maidservant or cattle, because "you were a servant in the land of Egypt." Or consider (Deut. 15:13-15): The slave is not to go out empty-handed when he is set free after his seventh year, for you were a slave in the land of Egypt; or (Deut. 24:17-18): You are not to pervert justice for the stranger or pawn the widow's garment, for you were a stranger in Egypt. The command is here grounded in God's act of deliverance. This argumentation is theologically very important. We see that the regulation of the relationship to the brother derives from the fact of the deliverance.

One could say much more about the theological substance of the commandments within Israel's history of faith. A comparison of Exod. 23:10-11 with Deut. 15:1 shows, for example, how the ancient custom of proclaiming a sacred fallowness, the proclamation of God's ownership of the land, could no longer be made in later times for purely economic reasons. The agrarian economy had been replaced by a money economy, and the deuteronomic commandment stems from this altered, economically new situation. The commandment transfers the ancient regulation into the contemporary money economy. What is new, however, is the urgency with which the command is addressed to the individual conscience: "You shall not harden your heart or shut your hand against your poor brother, but you shall open your hand to him, and lend him sufficient for his need, whatever it may be. Take heed, lest there be a base thought in your heart" (Deut. 15:7-9). The comparison of Exod. 23:4 with Deut. 22:1 ff. is also instructive. Whereas the old commandment required one to look after the stray domestic animal even of one's enemy, Deuteronomy changes the wording by substituting "brother," for "enemy"!

As we conclude these remarks, there remains a question: Why should the brother be helped? Here the Old Testament expresses itself with stark realism. These commandments are unsentimental and sober: he is to be granted legal protection, to enjoy the benefit of the regulation, and quite simply to share in a certain material prosperity, to share in the most elementary gifts of God's blessing. First in value among the blessings of life is land ownership (the very important 25th chapter of Leviticus must be reviewed here). But it is significant that just here the human right of possession is again strangely broken. God owns the land. "You are strangers and sojourners with me" (Lev. 25:23).

The writing prophets, considered in the light of these ancient laws, lived in a later culturally and religiously dissolute time. This time had loosed itself almost completely from the ancient patriarchal regulations. Men were enlightened and lived, at least in the cities, in luxury. The economic structure of their time was predominantly capitalistic; in any case large landed estates had suppressed the patriarchal economy of small farms. To this emancipated society the prophets declared with incomparable passion that Yahweh was keeping his commandments in force. It is quite wrong to understand the prophets as social reformers. On the contrary, they proclaimed the ancient laws in their time; they actualized them, without worrying whether they could still be observed fully. One theme is conspicuously prominent in this respect for almost all the prophets: the question about brotherhood is decided primarily in legal decision-making. In the way the community, acting as a legal body at the city gate, administers justice, it reveals whether it thinks and acts in a brotherly way. But again it is God's will for justice; God does not forfeit his sovereign right over Israel. The statements of the prophets that describe Yahweh's kindly concern for the poor are wonderful. Yahweh is guarantor for the poor; he reserves to himself their defense. The "social" message of the prophets is only one aspect of their primary proclamation, namely Yahweh's coming. God will come into history, and the poor will then be sheltered by him.

Isaiah (14:28-32) gives us a view into a time of especially sanguine political projects. A foreign delegation is in Jerusalem, and in every sidestreet people are asking themselves what answer will be given to the envoys. Isaiah takes up this question: "What will one answer the messengers of the nations? 'The Lord has founded Zion, and in her the afflicted of his people find refuge.' "

This care God has for the poor is expressed again by those who look for a messiah. Yahweh's anointed, who will carry out God's will on earth, will look after the poor and see them righted. In that the ancient ideas about the king's responsibility to provide for the poor are taken up. In one of the royal psalms there is held up to the king an ancient image of the royal provider for the poor. "For he delivers the needy when he calls, the poor and him who has no helper. He has pity on the weak and the needy, and saves the lives of the needy. From oppression and violence he redeems their life; and precious is their blood in his sight" (Ps. 72:12-14). In these words we have the most complete picture of brotherhood in the realm of the Old Testament. Yahweh's anointed is the guarantor and the surety for all who suffer.

II

"Behold, you have instructed many, and you have strengthened the weak hands. Your words have upheld him who was stumbling, and you have made firm the feeble knees" (Job 4:3-4). With these words Eliphaz appeals to Job's insight, and at the same time he draws thereby a beautiful picture of responsibility for one's neighbor. The Old Testament does not know our distinction between words and deeds. Rather, it attributes the greater significance to the word. To find the right word at the right moment is one of a person's highest duties. The book of Job gives examples of that in every chapter. Job's friends have come from afar, for something must be said in the presence of this misfortune. Such a catastrophe puts all who hear of it in a state of confession, as the book of Job shows in another passage. God listens to these conversations, indeed he makes sure that the right things are said (Job 42:7). We see, therefore, that there was in Israel a duty of witness to an erring or tempted brother.

Here one must recall the story of Joseph and its climax (Gen. 50:19-20), when after repeated conflicts Joseph finally speaks. Previously Joseph had treated his brothers strictly and graciously. Then, however, after the death of their aged father, when the bad conscience and the anxiety of the brothers rose once more, Joseph found the right and only acceptable word: "Am I in the place of God? As for you, you meant evil against me; but God meant it for good." This statement must be understood programmatically. Joseph defines in it first his relation to God and then that of the brothers. It is ultimately a comforting statement, for the brothers are to know that through all their wicked thoughts and deeds God had worked out his saving purposes. In this story Joseph himself is also an object of divine pedagogy as the one who was placed by God in a strict school; as one bowed low by God, he becomes God's instrument of instruction for his brothers.

In the realm of the cult we again meet this duty of guidance and instruction, but in quite a different form. The literary genus of the so-called "psalms of thanksgiving" reaches its height when the one who has experienced trouble and has known God's help in this need feels obliged to make this experience known to others. What help an individual has received from God is in some sense not his possession. It belongs instead to the community to which he must bear witness. The worst failure would be for him now to remain silent (Ps. 30:12; 32:8-11; 66:16, etc.). The concern here is certainly not for instruction, in the general sense of the word, or for the communication of some preserved wisdom about life; rather it is for a testimony in the strictest sense of the word, i.e., by means of a word that has been empowered by a preceding act of God.

We find the prophets were particularly insistent about this power of the helping word for the neighbor. The literary prophets of the eighth century show, in fact, an almost exclusive concern for the nation. But the story of Elisha and Naaman (II Kings 5) shows us how prophets again and again were available to the individual and his needs. In the story of Naaman, the shift from unrelenting severity to the greatest largeness of heart is significant. After Elisha has at first dashed Naaman's expectations to the ground, he responds to the two timorous questions about awkward exemptions with wonderful generosity. Without law, without casuistry, without an anxiously prescribed roadmap, he sends Naaman forth into the whole problematic of his life in the midst of the heathen.

The prophet whom we may characterize as the pastor par excellence is Ezekiel. He too, of course, is a prophet like Isaiah and Jeremiah, sent against nations and empires. But alongside that we find the single individual as an object of his prophetic calling.

> "Son of man, I have made you a watchman for the house of Israel; whenever you hear a word from my mouth, you shall give them warning from me. If I say to the wicked, 'You shall surely die,' and you give him no warning, nor speak to warn the wicked from his wicked way, in order to save his life, that wicked man shall die in his iniquity; but his blood I will require at your hand." (3:17-18)

This guardian office thus binds the prophet to every individual. He must follow the way of the individual and take him seriously in his quite particular, unique situation before God. That guardianship goes so far that the other's fate becomes that of the prophet himself; God identifies him in a certain sense with that other person. This mediating role of the prophet is deadly serious. The prophet's life, we might say his whole mental image, is bound to the "thou" of the other person. In the 18th chapter of his book, Ezekiel shows us how he follows theologically and pastorally the uncertainties of a person's life, with all its breakdowns and burdens.

In conclusion there is a consideration that could possibly seem to be totally unrelated to our theme. It can, however, suggest an aspect of it that we have not yet mentioned.

The Old Testament contains a host of stories of all genres and styles. They derive from storytellers, men, to be sure, but with a relationship to those things about which they talk. What is the attitude of these storytellers to those objects of theirs—these storytellers who are only men? Is one, when one reflects on this question, to wonder more that they do not treat their material heroically, or ideally, or that they do not condemn? For them not to have painted the pictures of Moses or David or Gideon in gold but to have left them completely in the believable framework of the human is a great achievement, and one that is unique in the literature of the ancient Near East. The Old Testament avoids on principle the danger of apotheosis.

But a cause for greater wonder perhaps is that they do not condemn either, even though they possess such radical standards. How easy it would have been to blacken the picture of Saul as a background for the story of David. But the narrator follows the path of the unhappy king with unreserved sympathy to the end. Or consider the frightful Jehu (II Kings 9–10). Why does the historian not break loose from him? Why does he not disqualify him morally and religiously? We observe again and again that the human image is never dishonored by these storytellers (neither angel nor beast—Pascal), and, we repeat, even though they have so penetrating a knowledge about the man and at the same time about God's judgment on this man. In these narrators we see a wonderful open-mindedness toward men, toward each man—but in the judgment something remains open. That is to say, the narrator speaks of the man as a brother. He maintains a hidden, ultimate solidarity with him before God; i.e., a shyness to separate himself from the man in question by a radical judgment. Theologically that means that these narrators do not think and speak legalistically. There rests, even on the stories of the worst scoundrels, something like an ultimate reserve, a proviso in which the narrator, so far as he is concerned, does not claim the final judgment. That means, we repeat, that he speaks of the man, even in extreme circumstances, as a brother. The narrators too accept the maxim that Joseph declared before his brothers: they do not stand in the place of God. One can say that their attitude would be impossible in the light of the law by itself. To think and speak about man in this way is possible only where everything human is placed in the light of God's forgiveness and grace. That is something quite different from philanthropy, and to realize the difference is to understand clearly that the Old Testament knows about true brotherhood.

18

STATEMENTS OF FAITH
IN THE OLD TESTAMENT
ABOUT LIFE AND ABOUT DEATH

(Lecture at the church conference in Leipzig on Pentecost 1934. First published in the General Evangelical-Lutheran Church Newspaper 71, 1938, cols. 826-834, in German.)

To approach our theme it is best for us to begin with one of those simple yet graphic stories that report a death. David's child, begotten in adultery, is dying. The king is praying in deep despair. The narrative in II Samuel 12 continues as follows:

> But when David saw that his servants were whispering together, David perceived that the child was dead; and David said to his servants, "Is the child dead?" They said, "He is dead." Then David arose from the earth, and washed, and anointed himself, and changed his clothes; and he went into the house of the Lord, and worshiped; he then went to his own house; and when he asked, they set food before him, and he ate. Then his servants said to him, "What is this thing that you have done? You fasted and wept for the child while it was alive; but when the child died, you arose and ate food." He said, "While the child was still alive, I fasted and wept; for I said, 'Who knows whether the Lord will be gracious to me, that the child may live?' But now he is dead; why should I fast? Can I bring him back again? I shall go to him, but he will not return to me." (vv. 19-23)

It is pleasing to see how the surpassing figure of the king is delineated even in such relatively insignificant characteristics. What David does is beyond the comprehension of

194

his courtiers. His resignation is so profound that he no longer lifts his hand for the simplest gesture of mourning. There can be an excess of grief, for which no expression of pain is any longer appropriate and before which a person is finally, indeed frightfully, sobered. Thus David returns speechless to his life. It is the only truly appropriate thing he can do in the full desolation of his situation. This small event is full of meaning. Here death is taken seriously as an absolute end. There is not so much as a quiet whisper of hope, not even the prospect of a reunion in death to give any comfort at all.

This is the view of death over wide stretches of the Old Testament, especially in the earlier period of Israel's history. It is *the* end, and once one has become aware of that, one must marvel at how little the Old Testament as a whole can say. How lively the religions become on just this point! How talkative and bold the ideologies! In the Old Testament there is nothing about that; no rite and no mythology bridges the deep chasm, neither a pathetic heroism nor a so-called conquest of death that would make it something innocuous. We might in fact believe that this is the way to demonstrate obedience to the reality of death, the way that sets one to thinking, a nonrhetorical sobriety in taking seriously what man experiences as the absolutely final. If one asks oneself, "What then is so special in the reports about the dying of devout people in the Old Testament that makes these stories have almost timeless validity?" then one must answer that it is just this sober, matter-of-fact quality, this final acceptance of death as being greater than every human will to live.

Now this conclusion is only a generality. We must now seek to understand this attitude from within. We may now ask why, in this view of death, life must not lose its balance even more; why it is that death really does not overshadow, as we moderns often feel it so intensively, the whole of life, so that in a certain sense the question about life unrolls in the presence of *its* majesty. We see nothing about that in this way. We do see, however, that death, insofar as it was not a sudden, early, evil death, was accepted with calm resignation and sometimes almost as a grace from God. "He died in a good old age, an old man and full of years" is what we read now and then in the Old Testament. One could dwell on the phrase "old and full of years." It obviously does not reckon from the start with the Faustian claim to an endless life, but rather with life as *limited, measured out* to man by God. Whether life was filled with joy or sorrow, one way or the other it has an end and therefore also an inner awareness of the coming end. There is also a condition of satiety, a point at which what God has measured out is finished; and this is then the moment when death occurs. There is thus something like a fulfillment of God in the coupling of the terms "old" and "full of years." One does not come without the other, neither old and still unsatiated, or not satisfied, i.e., "fed up" and despairing yet still not old. Both, however, old and full of years, constitute the full measure of human life, the fulfillment of what God had placed in the specific life.

That is important in two respects for our consideration. First, we will hear statements later about an abysmal despair in the presence of death, witnesses of a passionate struggle against death. We can say here already that they are not expressions of that Faustian drive for endless life, which no joy can satiate, no happiness satisfy. That is, they do not express that claim to endless life that *men* assert, but rather something quite different. And second, death is here obviously seen very closely together with life. Better, it is evaluated completely from the vantage point of life. It is not absolute, not the threatening majesty somewhere at the end, but rather a relative thing. We just observed that. Whoever dies old and full of years does not experience death as an enemy standing on the other side of life, but rather as a seal of God's fulfillment in his life.

Now we must quickly add that we are far from having made everything clear. Even when death came to an old man, he did not experience it completely without a sting. And how about the innumerable cases when death came wildly and apparently senselessly to the young who were not yet satisfied with life? Surely then it troubled and disturbed men as only men can be disturbed by death. We could in that connection hear from the Old Testament a loud choir of those in earnest about death.

"Man that is born of woman is of few days, and full of
   trouble. He comes forth like a flower, and withers;
he flees like a shadow, and continues not." (Job 14:1-2)
As for man, his days are like grass;
he flourishes like a flower of the field;
for the wind passes over it, and it is gone, and its place
   knows it no more. (Ps. 103:15-16)
The grass withers, the flower fades,
when the breath of the Lord blows upon it;
surely the people is grass." (Isa. 40:7)
When thou hidest thy face, they are dismayed;
when thou takest away their breath, they die
and return to their dust. (Ps. 104:29)

Those were the statements of a prophet, a wise man, and a singer of psalms; and they resemble each other in *one* thing completely. Death is in God's hand; *he* sends it. If God hides his face, man decays; man lives from the fact that God's grace lights his way. And what was veiled here, spoken more allusively and suggestively, is expressed openly in the 90th Psalm. It belongs to the most threatening words the Old Testament knew how to speak about death.

For a thousand years in thy sight
   are but as yesterday when it is past,
   or as a watch in the night.
Thou dost sweep men away; they are like a dream,
   like grass which is renewed in the morning:
in the morning it flourishes and is renewed;
   in the evening it fades and withers.
For we are consumed by thy anger;
   by thy wrath we are overwhelmed.
Thou hast set our iniquities before thee,
   our secret sins in the light of thy countenance.
For all our days pass away under thy wrath,
   our years come to an end like a sigh. . . .
Who considers the power of thy anger,
   and thy wrath according to the fear of thee? (vv. 4-11)

Now we see, to be sure, more clearly than we did before, that death is not considered as something independent, as some kind of anonymous majesty, but rather as a free act of God. Above all, death is not an independent entity, insofar as it is seen completely and exclusively from the vantage point of *life*. It is the disturbance of our relationship to God in *life*. The story of the Fall has already said this, that man's fear before God and his shame are the external consequences of an inner, disturbed relationship of man to God. This continual readiness he shows to be affrighted before his own creator, and even more, this enigmatic rupture that goes through our life, the fact that we are ashamed of our own bodies, this is not original and created, but is God's judgment on men for an original sin in which we all share. And now we must speak further about the secret concern with which the man of the Old Testament viewed even physical sickness as a sign of that *one* disturbance at the root of their whole existence, including that remarkable animosity against the physician in a passage of II Chronicles (16:12) that is so consistent. For if God is the creator of our bodies, who is more competent than he to care for bodily afflictions? Was it not a lack of faith and a misapprehension of the profound depth of the actual damage for a man to run to the doctor and toss to the wind that lapidary statement that had been given to the community of the Old Covenant, "I am the Lord, your healer"? (Exod. 15:26).

Now we see that our earlier conclusion, that in the Old Testament death has no independent majesty, must be expanded to include the fact that *life* too is not some objective matter that is at least somewhat available to man; life comes from God. Life is a gift to man, as we read in the book of Job: "If he should take back his spirit to himself, and gather to himself his breath, all flesh would perish together, and man would return to dust" (34:14-15). We could translate this sentence, which in itself is simple enough, even more simply and say that in the Old Testament life belongs to God. That question, therefore, that is so familiar to us, that question asked by autonomous men about the "meaning of life" and the "problem of death" is unknown in the Old Testament. According to it the meaning of life is that man belongs to God and serves him, and the problem of death (we seek in vain in the Old Testament for a convenient formula) is intimately mixed up with the question of human guilt. There is much mystery involved. One does not take the measure of death or rationally comprehend it, but still one does understand it ultimately: "For we are consumed by thy anger; by thy wrath we are overwhelmed."

By saying that life belongs to God we have affirmed something only very general for Old Testament thought. One must now reflect on the story of creation that ventured to touch in faith on the mystery of the planting of divine life in the body of man. One must further reflect on the immediate consequence of the statement about God's right of ownership with respect to life, namely, that murder is a sin against God. Not for man's sake, not because of some human law is murder a crime. Murder is a crime because it is against God's property and creature (Gen. 9:6).

On the basis of this and other texts we could say much more, and still it would always be possible, indeed even probable, for us to misunderstand in a modern sense our statement that life belongs to God. We could think, for example, that life is something mysterious and holy and ultimately derived from God, but for the present a kind of immanent power with its own legitimacy, some objective given for man. No. When we said life belongs to God, we meant that God lays claim to man's obedience and that man has life only in conformity with God's will. That sounds at first highly illogical and at variance with what we said before. We suspect that a completely different conception of life, a spiritual one, has been introduced. But that is not so. Listen to these statements from Moses's great farewell address to his people (Deut. 30:15-19):

"See, I have set before you this day life and good, death and evil. If you obey the commandments of the Lord your God

> which I command you this day, by loving the Lord your
> God, by walking in his ways, . . . then you shall
> live. . . . But if your heart turns away, and you will not
> hear, . . . I declare to you this day, that you shall perish;
> you shall not live long in the land. . . . I call heaven and
> earth to witness against you this day, that I have set before
> you life and death, blessing and curse; therefore choose life,
> that you and your descendants may live."

How strange is the talk there of life and death! Not at
all as though the listeners did not already have both, not
at all as though they were people who found themselves
more or less halfway between the entrance to life and the
entrance to death! No, they are addressed as people, *who,
in the moment when they hear God's word are for the first
time brought to the decision about life and death.*

When hearing God's word! That is the simplest
impression we have from the Old Testament, that there
an entire people was busy with God's word. Certainly not
busy to their own credit, often despairing of the word and
indeed opposing it, but still busy with it and kept alive by
it! What all does the Old Testament say here and there of
fright and joy *except* about the fact that the living God has
condescended to speak! For God's word is not an empty
word to you, says Moses simply and clearly in his farewell
speech, but *it is your life.* Those periods in Israel's history
when God's word was rare in the land, were dismal and
dead in retrospect. Exactly so does the individual cleave
with his whole physical condition in life to the fact that
God speaks to him: "My rock, be not deaf to me, lest if thou
be silent to me, I become like those who go down to the
Pit" (Ps. 28:1). In this connection we think of the
well-known commandment, "Honor your father and your
mother, that your days may be long in the land which the
Lord your God gives you." We should not timidly remove
this rider as something not quite so elevated, but rather
we should recognize the great fact that it sets the decision
about actual, physical life within the question of
obedience or disobedience to God. To hear God's word is
life, and life lived in disobedience is forfeit before God.
Thus, one of the shrillest threats in all prophecy in the

Old Testament is the one Amos gave when he prophesied a hunger for God's word:

> "Behold, the days are coming," says the Lord God, "when I will send a famine on the land; not a famine of bread, nor a thirst for water, but of hearing the words of the Lord. They shall wander from sea to sea, and from north to east; they shall run to and fro, to seek the word of the Lord, but they shall not find it." (8:11-12)

With that we would, generally speaking, have pursued one line of thought to its end. Life and death are not in themselves absolute, immanent data; neither the one nor the other is autonomous, but man receives life or death in his decision about heeding the word of God.

We do not have to cite parallels in the history of religions. How strange the ways in which religions of all times have tried by magic or mystery to win union with life; how constant the idea that life itself is to be understood as a mystery or sacred force! How coolly and clearly the Old Testament rejects this madness: "Man does not live by bread alone, but . . . by everything that proceeds out of the mouth of the Lord" (Deut. 8:3). This final statement of the Old Testament about life, which we have drawn as a conclusion, is *not* its final word about death.

We have first to bring to mind a few statements from the psalms of complaint in the Old Testament. They do not ameliorate the darkness and severity of the Old Testament's view of death; rather, they greatly increase it.

Hezekiah prays in great distress: "I said, I shall not see the Lord in the land of the living. . . . For Sheol cannot thank thee, death cannot praise thee; those who go down to the pit cannot hope for thy faithfulness. The living, the living, he thanks thee" (Isa. 38:11, 18-19).

We read the same thing now and then in the Psalter, especially in Psalm 88: "Thou hast put me in the depths of the Pit, in the regions dark and deep. . . . Is thy steadfast love declared in the grave. . . . Are thy wonders known in the darkness, or thy saving help in the land of forgetfulness?" (vv. 6 and 11-12).

These are certainly the most gloomy words about death in the Old Testament. They state bluntly that in death a man leaves the living relationship with God; the dead are outside the realm of Yahweh's worship that enlivens and heals them, and that is the profound bitterness of death.

God is a god of the living. That statement in the Old Testament has a very particular meaning. The living realm of the worship established by God has its limits. Life and duration in the light of God were promised to the *community*; but when the individual used up his allotted share in Yahweh's grace, he departed in death from this divine realm of life.

I want to refer once more to the submission and obviousness with which these men hold to just that which God has offered and allotted to them. Unless God first abolishes these limits, they do not autocratically transgress them. And there is one thing more. "Death does not praise thee." Death is, so to speak, completely deprived of divinity; faith in the Old Testament has stripped it radically of any numinous quality. *Mors janua vitae* (Death, the door to life) is not from the Old Testament! Death is not the door that opens by itself to the future life, and certainly not to an increase of life on the basis of consecrated mysteries one has received. To express it in more modern terms, the Dionysiac aspects of death become superstitious in the presence of the living God. One could say that Novalis in his hymns to the night completely abandoned the biblical, Christian faith in God. "Blessed be the eternal night; blessed be the eternal sleep." "I sense the regenerating flood of death; I live by day with faith and pluck, and die the nights in holy glow."—Death does not praise thee!

And now we take a great jump to the dialogues in the book of Job, where another atmosphere engulfs us. We see a person caught in a struggle of quite foreign format. We will do well not to understand too quickly what is being fought there beneath curse and entreaty, prayer and blasphemy, as our own; not to classify it too nimbly as an ancient version of one of our modern religious titanisms. What do we have? Job is no longer in the community; he has fallen from the certainty of being supported by the faith of the community. We could say he is an enlightened man; and out there in his frightful isolation, in the thin, frosty air of a religiosity without community or history, he suffers distresses of absolutely primeval dimensions. All of that was set in motion by his external fate; he is deathly sick, his community life is ruined, and he is at the threshold of death. Here at this final, small margin of his life, everything is enacted. What faith he might once have had is ruined for him. He has nothing left of the wonder of his forebears at the gracious revelation of God's will, nothing at all. What he sees, and indeed with outrage, is God's complete freedom and power with men.

> How can a man be just before God?
> If one wished to contend with him,
>   one could not answer him once in a thousand times . . .
> —who has hardened himself against him, and
>   succeeded?—
> he who removes mountains, and they know it not, . . .
> I shall be condemned; . . .
> If I wash myself with snow,
>   and cleanse my hands with lye,
> yet thou wilt plunge me into a pit,
>   and my own clothes will abhor me.

We hear that argument as a reality we cannot easily contest. This fact only may seem remarkable to us, namely, that Job does not for an instant, as we like to say, doubt God's existence. God's *reality* and action do not escape him. Quite the contrary! Job has never felt God so effectively as in this struggle. But God's activity eludes any believable logic; God seems purely arbitrary to him, and that arbitrariness has all the marks of the numinous, that is, God is a demon. Listen to another part of Job's complaint.

> "Oh that thou wouldest hide me in Sheol,
>   that thou wouldest conceal me until thy wrath be past,
>   that thou wouldest appoint me a set time, and remember
>   me! . . .

"All the days of my service I would wait,
  till my release should come.
Thou wouldest call, and I would answer thee; . . .
"But the mountain falls and crumbles away,
  and the rock is removed from its place; . . .
  so thou destroyest the hope of man." (Job 14:13-19)

What is that? An idea flashes in these gloomy statements: could God not take care of Job, keep him in mind perhaps beyond death? An ardent hope has risen in him, but he puts it to rest in profound resignation. In this, something of Job's innermost concern comes to light that is almost buried by the eruptions of his despairing soul. Job is interested in God and only in God; he woos him, asks about him, cannot die with this image of God in his heart. God knows that distant recollection of the faith of Job's forebears still binds Job and gives him no rest. It is a secret obligation to the living God, of which he is no longer conscious. Indeed, it is true that the cursing and blaspheming Job maintains God's interest against his friends. He *cannot* die until the affair between himself and the omnipotent and free God is clarified. His concern is not death itself, but this, that God, his God, has disappeared behind an ugly face of the most frightful arbitrariness. That brings him to knock at the gates of death, something almost unheard of in the Old Testament. If the matter is not settled *here* (he is about to die, after all), then God will somehow and somewhere beyond this life again be *his* God. "O earth, cover not my blood, and let my cry find no resting place. Even now, behold, my witness is in heaven, and he that vouches for me is on high . . . my eye pours out tears to God, that he would maintain the right of a man with God" (Job 16:18-21).

That is quite a new sound! The surety *(Bürge)* is a term in family law in the Old Testament. It is the closest relative in each instance who must assume the obligation in the case of impoverishment or indebtedness. There thus suddenly opens before Job a great prospect: God is his closest relative. That statement is ventured theologically in an act of ultimate despair, for there is that other, arbitrary God, who will not be flatly denied. So Job turns in mad overstatement to God against God.

He is calmer and more secure in his next monologue. "Oh that my words were written! Oh that they were inscribed in a book! Oh that with an iron pen and lead they were graven in the rock for ever! For I know that my Redeemer lives, and at last he will stand upon the earth; and after my skin has been thus destroyed, then without my flesh I shall see God" (Job 19:23-26).

That is certainly the most mysterious passage in Job's struggle. He had been concerned not with death, but with God and a return to his own personal relationship to him. And then it had suddenly come to him that death was not the ultimate power. It is possible that Job is not thinking of an eternal life, a resurrection, but only of a redeeming statement, a justification somehow and somewhere beyond this life. In that case, his concern and the comfort he found would be even greater for us, because we would then see more clearly how little that passage is actually concerned with the "problem of death." Job, separated externally from the devout community, takes this path in stern loneliness; the theology of the community did not direct him to it. On the very small bridge of his faith he accepted the venture and found the certainty that this free and omnipotent God was indeed *his* God in whom he could trust.

Others too, in the community of the Old Covenant, have taken this path in a similar way without knowing that others were on it too. It is remarkable how continually the voices of faith in the Psalter resound about death. "Bless the Lord, O my soul' . . . who forgives all your iniquity, . . . who redeems your life from the Pit" (Ps. 103:2-3). "I shall not die, but I shall live, and recount the deeds of the Lord" (118:17). The declarations become fuller and fuller, and more and more confident; the facts close in more and more closely about them; they oscillate about them more and more directly, carried first of all, to be sure, more by a surmise of faith that the community of life given by God cannot be broken suddenly from the

205

outside. So we read in Psalm 16: "Thou dost not give me up to Sheol, or let thy godly one see the Pit. Thou dost show me the path of life" (vv. 10-11).

That is certain, though nothing is known. The prayer does not say, "there is a life after death," but rather, "Thou dost not give me up to Sheol." Perhaps he is thinking first of all only of the impossibility that a sudden death could destroy his union with God; and yet, the certainty that has been granted to him reaches much farther than that. Psalm 73 shows that in the most wonderful way. The suppliant is profoundly troubled: "My feet had almost stumbled, my steps had well nigh slipped. For I was envious of the arrogant, when I saw the prosperity of the wicked . . . they have no pangs" (vv. 2-4).

This suppliant is somewhat related to Job: Where now is God's promise? His life is so threatened that he simply perceives nothing more of God's grace. A sober look at the way the lives of the devout and the godless go disproves the great statements of God. "When I thought how to understand this, it seemed to me a wearisome task" (v. 16). That is a beautiful word of touching candor. And now comes something quite surprising and apparently quite unmotivated.

> Nevertheless I am continually with thee;
>   thou dost hold my right hand.
> Thou dost guide me with thy counsel,
>   and afterward thou wilt receive me to glory.
> Whom have I in heaven but thee?
>   And there is nothing upon earth that I desire besides
>   thee.
> My flesh and my heart may fail,
>   but God is the strength of my heart and my portion for
>   ever. (vv. 23-26)

One will be unable to contradict the one who refuses to follow this declaration, who refuses suddenly to discard everything that sober observation has taught him. And yet we believe that God granted this unknown suppliant to say something ultimate about life and death from the side of God. It is basically that which we have seen all along. Neither life nor death are objective powers; faith cannot perceive them as anything standing the least bit independently next to God. Whoever takes God seriously knows that both rest in him and are subject to his decree. No sooner has our psalmist grasped this than he is quite confident and comforted, for to take God seriously means for him to take seriously God's promise of grace. This grace cannot fail; and for this fellowship in life that has been prepared by God there can be no death in the sense that this death, as some unforeseen accident, could make God's grace of no effect. No, that cannot happen to God. "Thou dost guide me with thy counsel, and afterward thou wilt receive me to glory." God has now and then "carried off" a person. Enoch was carried off; Elijah was carried off. This power to receive a person into a completely different realm of life beyond this one has always been credited to God. Death was no barrier to God's power. In Israel, however, one did not know that such a thing as a metaphysical legitimacy would become operative for every man. The suppliant of Psalm 73 also did not postulate that on his own in the name of man or in the name of life. If we thought that, we would misunderstand everything. He did something quite different. He cast himself completely on God's promise, on his promise of salvation, of which he was confident that no outside disturbance could cause it to fail. Thus the illumination is fully appreciated, that faith in God's salvation encloses an ultimate security, a security so unconditioned that it carries a person beyond the threshold of death and lets him remain in the community of God's life. It does this in and of itself, without that being its direct purpose.

Do not ask me to delimit this faith against every human speculation about the Beyond or against other ideologies of a mythological or magical nature. Faith is cogently simple and sober. For us, to be sure, all of whom start from somewhat speculative and even mythological postulates, it may not be quite so easy to see the entire greatness of this simplicity and sobriety.

Wellhausen once propounded the amazed question,

how was it possible that such religiously motivated and sincere men could have lived so long without hope in a continuation of life after death? We can now understand this fact, perhaps an astonishing one in the history of religions, and we can dispose of the question as irrelevant. For we saw precisely this, that the Old Testament is not concerned with a larger or smaller need for the continuation of life after death, not with the possibility that men should lay claim to it or autocratically take it as their own, but rather that man is completely directed to God's will. And in this respect the people of the Old Testament waited resignedly; but their wait had a most fundamental meaning, for in waiting they *learned* to see life and death just as we have pictured them, as the free gift and ordinance of the living God. But, of course, there is something in Wellhausen's question; one might have some thoughts about this period of waiting. There was a group of significant theologians in the nineteenth century who liked to speak a great deal about the economy of God with the community of the Old Covenant. One of their chief concerns was to penetrate what God might have intended with ancient Israel; and they believed they knew a great deal about God's principles of education, his reasons for doing this and not that. Today we can no longer completely agree. We think those men knew perhaps a little too much about God's intentions for the world. But this period of waiting, this absence of a tangible hope in a continuation of life, is a point to which we can say the following: It is as though God has first given his people all of this life, and the commandments of the Old Testament contain indeed God's will for this life, in an intensity about which the Christian community no longer has any idea at all. Here the question about God's relationship to this world and to man was not relativized in the interests of a future; there was no Beyond, looking forward to which one was continually tempted to postpone and remove the content of every unsettling fact. Rather, there was the earth and man, earnestly received from God, with no way out. Did that not have to be pointed out once? Was it not *necessary* to show once that every belief in the Beyond that bypasses God's will for the Here and Now is simply disobedience? We venture to show that it was necessary and that the Old Testament did so. We have seen that God, in his freely gracious will, nevertheless did not rest in offering man a fellowship in life beyond death; but we receive it, if we have understood the Old Testament correctly, as a great miracle from his hand.

In what precedes, we have evidently interpreted the declarations of faith in the Old Testament on the basis of their own content. Without speaking of the new life that has been granted to us through the resurrection of Jesus Christ, we have spoken of a faith, of which, after a superficial look, one could think that it is no longer ours. And yet one cannot, as a Christian, read these testimonies in the Old Testament to the true harshness of death and to the true life of obedience to God, without relating them to Jesus Christ. They all point, each in its own way, to his works and fulfillment. Indeed his judgment and salvation are already present in them.

19

PSALM 90

(Manuscript of a lecture at a public meeting of the Heidelberg Academy of Sciences in Freiburg im Bresgau, February 1963.)

It is not necessary to establish that a clean, scientific interpretation of religious poetry entails particular difficulties. And how much better off is the interpreter of western poetry; for in Near Eastern, at least ancient Near Eastern, poetry the individual poem is not at all, as we are almost matter-of-factly accustomed to assume it is, the direct expression of personal feeling and experience. The reason for this can be seen in the origin of this poetry and its proximity to the cult. For us, the man Goethe and his experiences are an indispensable key to understanding his poetry. But even if we knew all the details in the life of the poet who composed the book of Job, I doubt that knowledge would give us a chance of understanding his poetry better. The poetic forms he used betray at every step their sacred origin or otherwise conventional forms. I consider it a great misunderstanding, therefore, when this poetry is considered by the present day as autobiographical, a kind of personal confession. Its content is not the modern quest for the meaning of suffering either. I mention that because one doubtless needs a certain training and practice to read such poems properly and not to see in their statements, complaints, or confessions the very same problems familiar to us. Much sounds uncannily modern, but the interpreter is lost if he lets himself be guided by his modern way of proceeding. When an ancient Near Eastern poet, a psalmist, a man whom we think of as being caught in unimaginably profound, dead serious, social and cultic systems says "I," it is most doubtful that he means the same thing as a modern poet does. Often enough he intends a general, inclusive, collective I. His intention is not at all to express what only he could express in that way and no other has yet expressed. On the contrary, he includes the others also in his "I"; through him there speaks not only the isolated individual, but rather mankind on a much more inclusive basis than that of a single individual. In the fullness of the experience from which he speaks, he transcends the atomized, isolated, modern individual. Obviously, these presuppositions make it considerably more difficult to ascertain what the specific, special, and unique characteristics of ancient Near Eastern poetry are.

It is understandable that it took a long time before a scientific, really appropriate method was found for interpreting the psalms, especially a standard for suitably classifying the 150 psalms. It is clear that here all modern standards and classification systems are to be held off. Research on the psalms has traveled many wrong roads precisely in its short-circuited evaluation of them from the standpoint of an extremely subjective lyricism. Also, ancient Greek terms like odes, hymns, elegies, which have been applied to them, have quickly proved to be useless. In this situation it was H. Gunkel who at the beginning of this century set research on the psalms on a completely new foundation. In its essential points it has proved to be reliable until the present day, in spite of many modifications in its details. Gunkel began with the fact that these poems were not "literature" in antiquity; instead, each one had a definite function in life, in the public life. Indeed, until the contrary is proved, they were used especially in the realm of the great sacred institutions of the cult, the court, and jurisprudence. These institutions were the great regulatory powers in the life of ancient Israel. They stamped the style of all official statements and created a very definite stylistic convention. I am referring to Gunkel's famous question about the "Sitz im Leben" (the place in life), with which he approached every poem of ancient Israel. That enabled him to classify the large number of psalms into a much smaller number of genres, according to "the place in life" by which they were designed. The individual psalm of thanksgiving, for example, is to be understood from the situation of a vow that had to be fulfilled, the song of national complaint from a worship service of fasting on the occasion of a calamity in the land, etc. The powerful force of style in these poems cannot be overestimated. Genres can be separated from their place in life, i.e., one learned to speak the psalm at home, outside the sacred institutions. The genres, in other words, were used privately. But it is interesting that the genre retained all its characteristics and traditional topics even where the force of style of its place in life was gone. The conventional form is scarcely to be disturbed. There were, of course, possibilities for variation, which are particularly interesting in view of the overpowering force of the style. Genres could finally disappear, as Gunkel readily admitted, and I want to speak now about one such process of decay in a genre.

I invite you to follow an interpretation of the 90th psalm, which, of course, can deal only with particularly characteristic passages of this poem. The linguistic aspect of the matter, that contains a few unpleasant difficulties, must be completely set aside.

We are concerned with the only psalm ascribed to Moses. These attributions of authorship were added to the psalms so much later that they have no authoritative value for us. We do not know the traditions or considerations from which they derive. That this great psalm can be connected especially well with some person like Moses is of course a modern judgment. The psalm is many centuries, indeed more than half a millennium, younger than Moses.

"Lord, thou hast been our dwelling place in all

generations" (v. 1). The first line makes fully and unambiguously clear to the expert the genre to which the psalm belongs. More than one person is speaking. The community begins with a recollection of benefit it had earlier experienced, which is at the same time, of course, a cry for the help and security which it had earlier received from God. We can compare the introit of Psalm 44: "We have heard with our ears, O God, our fathers have told us, what deeds thou didst perform in their days, in the days of old . . . with thy own hand."

Here too there is a "we" and the recollection of an experienced benefit. That is the traditional introit of the national song of complaint that had its place in the extraordinary worship service of fasting in time of war or drought or famine. Already Gunkel observed that the question "How long?" which we find in Psalm 90, verse 13, belongs inalienably to the formal language of this type of complaint song.

"Before the mountains were brought forth, or ever thou hadst formed the earth and the world, from everlasting to everlasting thou art God" (v. 2). The verse echoes a distant myth about a birth of the mountains, indeed about labor pains and travail of mother earth when she gives birth. We have here, for an instant, the perspective of a primeval, bizarre, mythical idea of the mother earth; it rhymes poorly with the specific Israelite idea of creation by the creative word as we know it from Genesis 1, for example. But echoes of that kind, in later poems, i.e., at the time when belief in the creation was completely secure, have no significance at all. At all times poets like to evoke the primeval, even in the garb of primeval ideas. In God's great address in the book of Job, a young text, God asks the rebel: "Who shut in the sea with doors, when it burst forth from the womb?" (Job 38:8). To place things like that on the theological gold balance would show false theological zeal. That is now only a matter of style. For the poet to indulge in such ancient conceptions, as, e.g., among other things, to use the very strange word for earth *(tebel),* is a sign of special, chosen style, nothing more. We will, however, have to recall this matter.

No, the passage is astonishing in quite a different respect. I said that national songs of complaint begin with a recollection—here too. But the remarkable fact is that the view goes all the way back to creation, and beyond that into the abyss of God's eternity. The view intended to fix the experience of salvation in history, but it now seems to have slipped out of history. It has nothing to which it can cling. Here something has happened, if one may say so. The statement about the shelter, the refuge, is not developed, for instead of sighting out the story of salvation with its comforting experiences, the idea of God's past activity becomes so overpowering in the poem that it clears away the ideas of the poem's original intent and directs it to the eternity of God. It is something quite different for me to remind myself (or God) of his help in ancient times, than it is for the thought of God's eternity to overtake me and oppressively impose itself on me. Thus, then, the thought of the protective relationship, with which Israel so often consoled herself, is first of all dropped. The recollection, instead of expressing consolation, opens the door to a whole chain of exceedingly somber reflections.

"Thou turnest man back to the dust, and sayest, 'Turn back, O children of men!' " (v. 3, a so-called synonymous parallelism). God himself is the cause of bleak transience. "A thousand years in thy sight are but as yesterday when it is past, or as a watch in the night" (v. 4). That is the way things are between man and God, and that, in the view of the poem, is a profoundly depressing aspect. Men are "like grass which is renewed in the morning: in the morning it flourishes and is renewed; in the evening it fades and withers" (vv. 5-6). But in vv. 7-9 a still more somber horizon appears: "We are consumed by thy anger; by thy wrath we are overwhelmed. Thou hast set our iniquities before thee, our secret sins in the light of thy countenance. For all our days pass away under thy wrath, our years come to an end like a sigh." (This translation is better than Luther's grandiose rendering, "We pass our years like gossip"—*hegeh* is a short muffled sound, thus "sigh.")

With that the poem has reached a new complication in

the relationship to God: sins are the most profound cause for the wretchedness of this relationship. The statement in v. 8 is accented strangely as an ascending synthetic parallelism: the emphasis lies on the words, "our secret sins in the light of thy countenance." And here it is difficult to be brief.

The modern man—excuse this simplification—tends plainly, especially where the religious is concerned, to accept responsibility only for that of which he is aware. He rejects liability for violations that he cannot at all recognize as such. In this the ancients, both Greeks and Israelites, thought quite differently. They were deeply troubled by the thought that a man in madness or any kind of misunderstanding of his situation before God could have "unknowingly" transgressed divine ordinances or encroached upon divine prerogatives. A community that is determined by archaic-sacred standards is concerned primarily, of course, about violating or overlooking certain rites. And it could set us thinking that precisely the politically active man, in ancient terms the king, was the one who by his activity stood in the zone of most extreme danger. Think, for example, of king Saul, who from time to time slipped from the guiding divine hand. With superhuman strength he set his face against the irrupting misfortune. Although subjectively he wanted the best, he became entangled in deeper and deeper infractions of inviolable, sacred ordinances, until he finally became engulfed in merciless despair. And with what retiring human sympathy does the narrator follow the face of the unhappy king! Our psalm must be dated much later than that, but it knows well enough about these things. It knows that a man should never presume to know the image God has of him, and that under all circumstances divine standards and not the judgments of men are decisive. It is concerned, then, in its way, with a wonderful readiness to be wrecked with all human wisdom before the deity.

"The years of our life are threescore and ten, or even by reason of strength fourscore; yet their span is but toil and trouble" (v. 10). There would not be much to say about this famous passage if there had not arisen, quite wrongly, some very remarkable misunderstandings from Luther's translation, as we will see at once. He translated it, "and if it is pleasant, still it is trouble and labor." Serious scholars have maintained that Luther here genially gave a new interpretation to the psalm; he set the negative Near Eastern attitude toward work over against the high esteem placed on it in the West. In the era of Hitler that became in popular literature part of the arsenal of polemic against the Old Testament. Now the glorification of work is a remarkably unrealistic and quite recent ideology with which we would not have to be concerned at all, if it had not so vehemently taken possession of this passage from the psalm and monopolized it. But a very simple philological consideration bars the way to all temptations to misunderstand the text. Luther found the word, work (labor), in the Vulgate. He understood it, however, not in the special modern sense, but rather in the closely related, middle-high German sense of toil or misery. We find it similarly in Deutero-Isaiah, "You have burdened me with your sins" (Isa. 43:24), and "the travail of his soul" (Isa. 53:11). It can be found in the language of many contemporary hymns of the church too. The conclusion, therefore, is that Luther caught precisely the bitter meaning of our passage.

Those are not, to be sure, popular insights. Thus the psalm continues: "Who considers the power of thy anger, and thy wrath according to the fear of thee?" (v. 11). Here the song seems to speak from a profound loneliness, which, as we must once more realize, does not properly belong to the genre of the national song of complaint. How terribly do men account themselves in their condition before God. How much they know about the captivities and alienation into which God has delivered mankind. What is it that man in this situation needs above all? The song draws the conclusion with great simplicity: "So teach us to number our days that we may get a heart of wisdom" (v. 12). That is what man lacks, a heart of wisdom. Wisdom in the Old Testament is something extremely sober. It is the knowledge of life and the art of living, the adaptation to all realities, to which belong also the realities of man's relationship to God. For man to know these things, God himself must help him, open his eyes, show him the reality of his relationship to God. For this reason the psalm says "teach us." Have you noticed that this is the first petition to arise from the song of complaint? Now we are conscious for the first time of how unnatural and conspicuous petition is in a national song of complaint, in that it comes only toward the end of the psalm. The resignation, however, was too burdensome. Let us say it calmly: God was too far from that realm of dark and bitter reflection, in which the psalm was moving, to be addressed. Now, however, the spell is broken; the psalm has at last found again the divine "thou," and there is scarcely a halt to the petitions.

> So teach us to number our days
>   that we may get a heart of wisdom.
> Return, O LORD! How long?
>   Have pity on thy servants!
> Satisfy us in the morning with thy steadfast love,
>   that we may rejoice and be glad all our days.
> Make us glad as many days as thou hast afflicted us,
>   and as many years as we have seen evil.
> Let thy work be manifest to thy servants,
>   and thy glorious power to their children.
> Let the favor of the Lord our God be upon us,
>   and establish thou the work of our hands upon us,
>   yea, the work of our hands establish thou it. (vv. 12-17)

In this sudden flood of requests, one statement in particular must occupy our attention: "Let thy works be manifest to thy servants, and thy glorious power to their children." What does that prayer mean? We have here to be circumstantial, for here, if I see correctly, is a pivotal point for understanding the entire psalm. I remind you that ancient Israel's faith was always related to an event in history in which God would manifest himself. To Israel, every form of philosophical speculation and religious mysticism was just as strange as the recourse to nonhistorical, mythical, primeval events. This faith arose from divine acts, from saving events of one kind or another, from appointments, foundations, and thorough supports; and it extended to one saving event and quite particular fulfillments that God has promised to Israel. The whole Old Testament is thus a single book of history, gigantic in its complexity; for the prophets too are concerned with history, namely, with its future. Whenever and wherever Israel set out to understand and express herself in the world before God (and the need for that arose often), she did so in a historical work of more and more powerful drafts of a theology of history. Israel had a phenomenal contact with history; her sensitivity in this direction is expressed in numerous individual conceptions that often enough cannot be made to agree with each other at all. In a word, Israel's faith *lived* from her view of God's activity in history. Wherever she kept that in view, she could endure much; wherever God's saving will disappeared on the horizon of history, Israel was plunged into profound troubles. It was easier for her when at times her image of God became distorted or took on incomprehensible and frightful characteristics, than when she lost sight of God's sovereignty completely.

And now let us once more try to understand our psalm against this background. Has it become clear to you that the psalm is really a stranger in the Old Testament? Already the beginning of the prayer appears in a peculiar light, in the way the traditional backward glance at earlier divine acts of salvation is missing, and the look at history found nothing to which it could cling; in the way it glided further and further back to the creation of the world and finally confronted in shock the eternity of God: "A thousand years in thy sight are but as yesterday when it is past, or as a watch in the night." Finally, of course, it is two quite different things for me to remember that God has helped in the past, or to consider that God is limitless and eternal and that this form of his divine being oppressively impresses man. How did this destruction of the traditional outline of prayer occur? Here there must have been a power at work that compelled this break in the style (and what does that mean for the continuation and conservatism of cultic forms!).

Now I must invite you once more to a short excursus.
We have in the Old Testament one book that with great
impressiveness exhibits in detail this situation of a total
loss of history. That work revolves both about this
bankruptcy of a faith that was based on saving facts and
also about the result of this catastrophic loss of history.
That book is Ecclesiastes. Its opening song, a poem of
monumental melancholy, contains fundamentally all of
that.

> Vanity of vanities, says the Preacher,
>   vanity of vanities! All is vanity.
> What does man gain by all the toil
>   at which he toils under the sun?
> A generation goes, and a generation comes,
>   but the earth remains for ever.
> The sun rises and the sun goes down,
>   and hastens to the place where it rises.
> The wind blows to the south,
>   and goes round to the north;
> round and round goes the wind,
>   and on its circuits the wind returns.
> All streams run to the sea,
>   but the sea is not full;
> to the place where the streams flow,
>   there they flow again.
> All things are full of weariness;
>   a man cannot utter it;
> the eye is not satisfied with seeing,
>   nor the ear filled with hearing.
> What has been is what will be,
>   and what has been done is what will be done;
>   and there is nothing new under the sun.
> Is there a thing of which it is said,
>   "See, this is new"?
> It has been already,
>   in the ages before us.
> There is no remembrance of former things,
>   nor will there be any remembrance
> of later things yet to happen
>   among those who come after. (vv. 2-11)

"There is nothing new under the sun!" That is the
provocative statement. And when men continue to assert
that, it is because of their narrowness and their short

memory. It also occurred earlier, in the times before our own. What must have happened if such a thing could be said in Israel where one previously had been forced again and again by new divine ordinances and contingencies to newer and newer theological conceptions of history! The historical passage of time, which for Israel was the place of repeatedly new saving events, has become an agony!

If, however, all life is set in an agonizing cycle, from which it cannot break free, then the question about God is quite a different one. And so we see the author of this book tastes from all areas of life, all phenomena in the living realm of man—work, culture, joy, comfort, marriage, riches, honor, poverty, piety, godlessness, wisdom, folly. All of it is illuminated by the question, where can a man in this life station himself? Where in all the shifting relativism, in this desperate cycle, is there a divine direction, a divine authority? Expressed in the author's words, "What is there for man from the hand of God?" Is not everything, even the loftiest exertion "a striving after wind"? And the answer is very resigned: "All this I have tested by wisdom; I said, 'I will be wise'; but it was far from me. That which is, is far off, and deep, very deep; who can find it out?" (7:23-24). He can lay hold of nothing that is genuine, so the question of man's relationship to God must be answered before one can answer the question about realities. "As you do not know the way of the wind, or how the bones grow in the womb of a woman with child, so you do not know the work of God who makes everything" (11:5). "I saw all the work of God, that man cannot find out the work that is done under the sun. However much man may toil in seeking, he will not find it out; even though a wise man claims to know, he cannot find it out" (8:17).

Have you heard how the question about God's activity is raised in both statements, exactly as it is in our psalm? It is the original question of the Old Testament. There is the question, but the answer has become quite different. God is not denied, nor is his activity. But his rule, his guidance in history, his providence in individual lives is buried in such deep secrecy that faith cannot reach it.

This is what is new and troubling. The preacher finds himself unable to say anything about this rule, which, as we have said, he basically does not dispute. And therewith man loses, as a logical consequence, his place in life, his rank in the world, his dignity, and his authority to act. That is the sorrow of the author of Ecclesiastes. If I may be permitted to use a somewhat risky slogan, I would say that man's relationship to the metaphysical ground of being that supports him wins tragic characteristics. That would be something originally quite foreign to the thought and faith of the Old Testament, insofar as one understands "tragic" to include a fated determination of man's existence, a limitation of his relationship to men and to God before whom he finds himself against his will. The older opinion, that the influence of popular Greek philosophy brought about this change, has been given up. We see today that the way to this skepticism was prepared long in advance in Israel. That makes the phenomenon even more interesting.

This brief reference to Ecclesiastes must suffice, but I think you also are satisfied to assume that our psalm derives from about the same intellectual and theological situation as Ecclesiastes. This loss of history, so exceptional in the Old Testament, is characteristic also of the 90th Psalm. What does the psalm say about God? That he is eternal, that men live under the judgment of this distant, hidden God, and that God's work, the glory of his saving activity, must be revealed to men. Only in that did the psalmist find consolation again. And how could the author of Ecclesiastes, who knew how to speak so movingly about the profound hiddenness of God's activity, have formulated his petition to God any other way than: "Let thy work be manifest to thy servants, and thy glorious power to their children"?

Having determined the theological position of the psalm, we have also opened the way to incorporate this poem into a somewhat wider context. I do not believe in the cultic situation from which this psalm is supposed to have come, as is once more asserted in the most recent large commentary on the Psalms. The psalm is much too reflective to be a cultic-liturgical text. Such far-reaching reflections about "our life" have no place in an actual national song of complaint. The need that is here lamented is different in kind from that of hostile invasion, pestilence, famine, or an invasion of locusts; it is much more basic than sorrow at God's hiddenness. Here, simply, the dimension of man's God-forsakenness comes into view. The genre of the national song of complaint, which gives the psalm, even in its present form, its unmistakable stamp, is accordingly to be understood only as an art form. It is no longer cultic, but a freely chosen literary figure which an unknown poet used for his poem. We know from the prologue of the grandson of Jesus Sirach that his grandfather transmitted not only traditional matters, but that he also augmented them by his own free creations—hymns, songs of thanksgiving, and others. Our psalm, then, belongs to that intellectual, theological phenomenon we call "wisdom." It is part of that very spiritual theology, remarkably separated from cult and saving history, the bearers of which we have to seek in the schools of wisdom. That means that our psalm is relatively young, and in my opinion it is certainly postexilic. We cannot fix the date of its writing any more precisely than that.

And now, if you will allow me, I will read you the psalm in its entirety, so that the poem and not the interpretation may have the last word.

> LORD, thou hast been our dwelling place
>   in all generations.
> Before the mountains were brought forth,
>   or ever thou hadst formed the earth and the world,
>   from everlasting to everlasting thou art God.
> Thou turnest man back to the dust,
>   and sayest, "Turn back, O children of men!"
> For a thousand years in thy sight
>   are but as yesterday when it is past,
>   or as a watch in the night.
> Thou dost sweep men away; they are like a dream,
>   like grass which is renewed in the morning:
> in the morning it flourishes and is renewed;
>   in the evening it fades and withers.

For we are consumed by thy anger;
  by thy wrath we are overwhelmed.
Thou hast set our iniquities before thee,
  our secret sins in the light of thy countenance.
For all our days pass away under thy wrath,
  our years come to an end like a sigh.
The years of our life are threescore and ten,
  or even by reason of strength fourscore;
yet their span is but toil and trouble;
  they are soon gone, and we fly away.
Who considers the power of thy anger,
  and thy wrath according to the fear of thee?
So teach us to number our days
  that we may get a heart of wisdom.
Return, O LORD! How long?
  Have pity on thy servants!
Satisfy us in the morning with thy steadfast love,
  that we may rejoice and be glad all our days.
Make us glad as many days as thou hast afflicted us,
  and as many years as we have seen evil.
Let thy work be manifest to thy servants,
  and thy glorious power to their children.
Let the favor of the Lord our God be upon us,
  and establish thou the work of our hands upon us.
  yea, the work of our hands establish thou it.